Ezra: Help

For the Restoration of the Temple

LESLIE ACHORD

FIRST EDITION

ISBN: 978-1-936989-46-1

Library of Congress Control Number: 2012935921

Published by
NewBookPublishing.com, a division of Reliance Media, Inc.
2395 Apopka Blvd., #200, Apopka, FL 32703
NewBookPublishing.com

Printed in the United States of America

Dedicated

To

Marilyn and Joseph,
my loving daughter and son

and

to those desiring to be restored
with God's help

and

In loving memory
of

Alma Jones
11-14-21 to 5-19-09

Ezra: Help

TABLE OF CONTENTS

FOREWORD

It is my desire to recapture for you how the Lord restored me, through the book of Ezra. I want to lead and guide you step by step to a place of restoration, wholeness and satisfaction. Ezra contains twenty-one chapters, which are meant to be read one chapter per day over a twenty-one day period. If you follow those instructions, I am confident that your life will never be the same.

I found myself in need of restoration because I refused to listen to simple instructions. I had come to a place of realization that my life wasn't all I had hoped it would be. I was rebellious and guilty of doing things my way. Looking back on my life, I noticed that things started going wrong the day I chose to rebel against the Lord. I came to know Jesus as my personal Lord and Savior when I was seven years old. Knowing I needed forgiveness, I chose to seek the Lord. I found a church that was close to my home and began to attend.

During this time, as I read the book of Ezra, the Lord impressed upon my heart that He wanted to restore me, the temple of the Holy Spirit (I Cor. 6:19, 20). He wanted to restore me, as He had restored the Temple in Jerusalem, after the Jews had been in captivity for seventy years. This captured my attention, because I knew I had been held in captivity to the sin in my life. I wanted to be restored more than anything else in the world. I had made many poor choices and was grateful the Lord was willing, and even desired, to fully restore me.

I am here today to tell you that He was faithful and wants to restore you. He has put it on my heart to write this book for that very purpose. His temple has been neglected and desolate for far too long. Come with me, and see that the Lord is good!

Isaiah 52:7-10

⁷ How lovely on the mountains
Are the feet of him who brings good news,
Who announces peace
And brings good news of happiness,
Who announces salvation,
And says to Zion, "Your God reigns!"

⁸ Listen! Your watchmen lift up their voices,
They shout joyfully together;
For they will see with their own eyes
When the LORD restores Zion.

⁹ Break forth, shout joyfully together,
You waste places of Jerusalem;
For the LORD has comforted His people,
He has redeemed Jerusalem.

¹⁰ The LORD has bared His holy arm
In the sight of all the nations,
That all the ends of the earth may see
The salvation of our God.

DAY 1

DESOLATE

Desolate: devoid of inhabitants and visitors: deserted;
Desert: to withdraw from or leave, usually without intent to return;
Synonym: abandon; to give up to the control
or influence of another person or agent.

The book of Ezra is about the restoration of the temple of God in Jerusalem. Today we are called the temple of God.

The Bible says:

I Corinthians 3:16-17

[16] Do you not know that you are a temple of God and *that* the Spirit of God dwells in you? [17] If any man destroys the temple of God, God will destroy him, for the temple of God is holy, and that is what you are.

Throughout this book we will learn from Israel's experience and example how to be restored with God's help, according to His perfect plan. Before the restoration can begin, however, we need to first understand what caused the destruction and why God allowed it to happen. By understanding this, we can make sure it doesn't happen again.

I have included the scriptures in this book, because I want you to see them for yourself.

II Chronicles 36:11-14

¹¹ Zedekiah was twenty-one years old when he became king, and he reigned eleven years in Jerusalem. ¹² He did evil in the sight of the LORD his God; he did not humble himself before Jeremiah the prophet who spoke for the LORD. ¹³ He also rebelled against King Nebuchadnezzar who had made him swear *allegiance* by God. But he stiffened his neck and hardened his heart against turning to the LORD God of Israel. ¹⁴ Furthermore, all the officials of the priests and the people were very unfaithful *following* all the abominations of the nations; and they defiled the house of the LORD which He had sanctified in Jerusalem.

Zedekiah, the king, was evil and rebellious. He was determined not to turn to the Lord God of Israel. He was very proud and refused to listen to the Lord. "He did not humble himself before Jeremiah the prophet who spoke for the Lord." King Zedekiah wanted to rule God's people *his* way, instead of God's way. The religious leaders and the people were also unfaithful to God. They were "following all the abominations of the nations." They had defiled the house of the Lord. Their continual lack of reverence and respect for God and His house caused the desolation.

Today, most people are experiencing desolation in one area or another in their lives. This is not now, nor has it ever been, God's plan for anyone. As you continue reading, take a deeper look at your own life and the choices you've made. Are those you've placed in leadership over you seeking the Lord for guidance? Have you defiled the temple of God? Are you conscientious about what you allow into your temple? Have you kept yourself holy and pure for His glory? In order to be restored, we need to look at ourselves and our choices.

This is not a time to focus on what others are doing.

After my grandmother passed away, the world became dark and desolate for me. I was a spiritual and an emotional mess. She had been the light in my world. She was the only Christian in my life. I knew she was in heaven, and I was very happy for her. But, I also knew I couldn't continue living my life without the Lord. I knew I needed my own relationship with Him. My grandmother once said to me, "I hope your grandfather and I won't be in heaven waiting for no one to show up." I then promised her my kids and I would make it. She knew I had walked away from the Lord when I was fifteen years old. The desolation I felt stirred up within me a hunger for God and biblical truths as never before.

Let's see how God tried to turn the Israelites around before their fall.

II Chronicles 36:15-16

¹⁵ The LORD, the God of their fathers, sent word to them again and again by His messengers, because He had compassion on His people and on His dwelling place; ¹⁶ but they *continually* mocked the messengers of God, despised His words and scoffed at His prophets, until the wrath of the LORD arose against His people, until there was no remedy.

This passage says that because of God's great compassion for His people and His dwelling place, the temple, He sent messenger after messenger to talk to them. However, no one was listening. They continually mocked His messengers, despised His words and scoffed at His prophets, until His wrath arose against them, until there was no remedy. He loved them, so He could not allow them to continue on this path of destruction. Their poor choices are what caused His wrath. They refused to listen to His messengers.

No one was praying for discernment (the ability to know right from wrong, good from evil, and truth from lies) regarding the words of the prophets. These messengers were not false prophets. They were His messengers speaking His words. The Lord was there with His people all along. He was talking to them through His prophets. Instead of listening, however, His people treated the prophets as if they were out of control.

Today, are we receptive to those whom God has sent to us? Are we listening to His messengers? Surely He is sending them, for we know He is the same yesterday, today and tomorrow. Are we too quick to dismiss those who think differently than we do? Are we considering what they are saying and whether or not it lines up with the Word of God? Are we considering the possibility that we are out of control? Looking at the world around us, I do believe more of us need to stop and take into consideration our own actions. Are we doing good or evil, in the sight of the Lord?

You can pray and ask Him to remind you of any words He has spoken to you through another person. When He does, you'll realize He speaks through ordinary people and has been there for you all along. When I did this, I realized how much I needed Him and how blessed I would have been if only I had listened. However, it is never too late to start listening. He is waiting for us to ask Him for help. This is the desire of His heart. He loves us.

What we are doing may appear to be good in our sight. However, if we are doing things our way, rather than seeking Him for counsel, the end result will be less than His best for us. In Proverbs, we read that success comes with much counsel. If we remember that He holds the future in His hands and wants us to be successful, we will be more likely to stop and pray before making any decisions. He knows the end result of every decision that comes our way before it happens. This information is available to us. All we have to do is pray for it and wait for His answer.

God couldn't stand to watch Israel defile His house any longer. He saw all that He was willing to see. You can read II Kings, Chapters 21-23, to see in more detail how they defiled the Temple. The desolation was caused by their actions and choices. They were no longer a people under God. They were doing things their way. In behaving that way, they stirred up the wrath of God.

Now, let's take a look at His wrath.

II Chronicles 36:17-23

[17] Therefore He brought up against them the king of the Chaldeans who slew their young men with the sword in the house of their sanctuary, and had no compassion on young man or virgin, old man or infirm; He gave *them* all into his hand. [18] All the articles of the house of God, great and small, and the treasures of the house of the LORD, and the treasures of the king and of his officers, he brought *them* all to Babylon. [19] Then they burned the house of God and broke down the wall of Jerusalem, and burned all its fortified buildings with fire and destroyed all its valuable articles. [20] Those who had escaped from the sword he carried away to Babylon; and they were servants to him and to his sons until the rule of the kingdom of Persia, [21] to fulfill the word of the LORD by the mouth of Jeremiah, until the land had enjoyed its sabbaths. All the days of its desolation it kept sabbath until seventy years were complete.

[22] Now in the first year of Cyrus king of Persia—in order to fulfill the word of the LORD by the mouth of Jeremiah—the LORD stirred up the spirit of Cyrus king of Persia, so that he sent a proclamation throughout his kingdom, and also *put it* in writing, saying, [23] "Thus says Cyrus king of Persia, 'The LORD, the God of heaven, has given me all the kingdoms of the earth, and He has appointed me to build Him a house in Jerusalem, which is in Judah. Whoever there is among you of all His people, may the LORD his God be with him, and let him go up!'"

Nebuchadnezzar's army walked away with all the articles and treasures of the house of God and the king. This was the Lord's way of protecting them for future use. He called the Temple "the house of God" twice, reminding Israel that it was His house and built for His glory.

The Temple was so defiled that God had it burned in order to purify it for future use. The wall of Jerusalem was broken down and the fortified buildings were burned, representing His protection being removed. All of the valuable articles that were left behind were destroyed.

The words that come to my mind are: "One nation, under God, indivisible with liberty and justice for all." However, in Israel we see a nation that replaced God with other gods. They were no longer living as though they were under God's authority. This caused them to fall and be carried away to a foreign land. Liberty and justice were exchanged for slavery and death. They became Nebuchadnezzar's servants.

Many of us have been carried away by worldly temptations that deceived and captured our minds. Money, possessions and pleasure took God's place. They became number one. It is not too late to turn back toward God and reclaim Him for ourselves.

This passage states that "the land had enjoyed its sabbaths." It rested every day for seventy years. The land was in anguish, caused by the sin of His people, and the blood and carnage left behind from King Nebuchadnezzar's army. This isn't the first time this happened. We read in Genesis that after Cain killed Abel, the Lord said to him, "The voice of your brother's blood is crying to Me from the ground" (Gen. 4:10). Considering this, you can now imagine the cries made by the blood of His people slain in Jerusalem. The Lord cleansed the land by fire and gave it seventy years to rest.

Let's look at the cause of another desolate time. The four hundred years of silence between the Old and New Testament. Following are the final words God spoke to the priests through Malachi, the prophet.

Malachi 1:6-11

⁶ " 'A son honors *his* father, and a servant his master. Then if I am a father, where is My honor? And if I am a master, where is My respect?' says the LORD of hosts to you, O priests who despise My name. But you say, 'How have we despised Your name?' ⁷ You are presenting defiled food upon My altar. But you say, 'How have we defiled You?' In that you say, 'The table of the LORD is to be despised.' ⁸ But when you present the blind for sacrifice, is it not evil? And when you present the lame and sick, is it not evil? Why not offer it to your governor? Would he be pleased with you? Or would he receive you kindly?" says the LORD of hosts. ⁹ "But now will you not entreat God's favor, that He may be gracious to us? With such an offering on your part, will He receive any of you kindly?" says the LORD of hosts. ¹⁰ "Oh that there were one among you who would shut the gates, that you might not uselessly kindle *fire on* My altar! I am not pleased with you," says the LORD of hosts, "nor will I accept an offering from you. ¹¹ For from the rising of the sun even to its setting, My name *will* be great among the nations, and in every place incense is going to be offered to My name, and a grain offering *that* is pure; for My name *will* be great among the nations," says the LORD of hosts.

This passage is very strong. It clearly reveals to us the hearts of the priests. The Lord says they despised His name, gave Him no honor and did not show Him any respect. He then repeats their very words: "How have we despised Your name?" The Lord clearly answers their question by saying, "You are presenting defiled food upon My altar." Their actions told Him they despised His table.

They were offering Him blind, sick and lame animals as sacrifices on His altar, when only the best animals were to be offered. Twice, He asks, "Is this not evil?" He then asks three more questions: Why haven't you offered such food to your governor? Would he be pleased with it? Would he receive you kindly?

Everyone knew the answers to these questions. He then calls Himself the Lord of hosts (angels). He is reminding them of who He is, since they had evidently forgotten. He continues, asking, "After offering such sacrifices will you then ask for My favor and for Me to be gracious to you and to receive you kindly?" He then shouts, "Oh, that there were one among you who would shut the gates, that you might not uselessly kindle fire on My altar!" What they were doing was not pleasing to God, nor was He willing to accept their offering.

The Temple priests were not pleasing to God at the end of the Old Testament. However, He says from the rising to the setting of the sun three things will happen. These were: His name will be great among all nations; in every place, there will be incense offered to His name (incense represents prayer); and pure grain will also be offered to His name.

We will now look at Israel after the four hundred years of silence. Let's read what Jesus had to say to the priests.

Matthew 23:13, 16a, 17a, 33-39

13 "But woe to you, scribes and Pharisees, hypocrites, because you shut off the kingdom of heaven from people; for you do not enter in yourselves, nor do you allow those who are entering to go in.

16 "Woe to you, blind guides

17 "You fools and blind men!

33 You serpents, you brood of vipers, how will you escape the sentence of hell?

34 **"Therefore, behold, I am sending you prophets and wise men and scribes; some of them you will kill and crucify, and some of them you will scourge in your synagogues, and persecute from city to city, 35 so that upon you may fall** *the guilt* **of all the righteous blood shed on earth, from the blood of righteous Abel to the blood of Zechariah, the son of Berechiah, whom you murdered between the temple and the altar. 36 Truly I say to you, all these things will come upon this generation.**

37 "Jerusalem, Jerusalem, who kills the prophets and stones those who are sent to her! How often I wanted to gather your children together, the way a hen gathers her chicks under her wings, and you were unwilling. 38 Behold, your house is being left to you desolate! 39 For I say to you, from now on you will not see Me until you say, 'BLESSED IS HE WHO COMES IN THE NAME OF THE LORD!'"

After the four hundred years of silence, Jesus was born in Bethlehem, as prophesied. He ministered for three years in Israel. During this time, He confronted the Pharisees regarding their hearts. He said they were shutting the kingdom of heaven for others to enter in, because they themselves refused to. He said they would kill, crucify, persecute and scourge some of the prophets, wise men and scribes He was sending. When He said this, He knew that He would be one of those who would be killed. He accused Jerusalem of killing and stoning the prophets the Lord had sent, and said that the guilt of all the righteous blood shed on earth would fall upon them.

It was the jealousy of the priests that kept the people away from Jesus. The Father first sent His servants, the prophets. He then sent His only begotten Son, His Servant. They killed some, but persecuted all of them. He states that He often wanted to gather their children the way a hen gathers her chicks under her wings, but they were unwilling. He shouts, "Behold, your house is being left to you desolate!"

The priests refused to listen to the prophets or the Son. He ends by saying they will not see Him until they shout, "Blessed is He who comes in the name of the Lord!"

Jesus' name is great among all nations. Prayer is being offered to His name all over the world. He is the pure grain offering, the Bread of Life. This is the bread eaten during communion, throughout the world.

Jesus is coming back for His bride, the church. She is to be found white as snow. He will return as King of Kings. We need to be ready.

The Lord has been faithful in keeping us safe. The loss of financial stability and peace in our lives could be His way of telling us to consider our ways. If we choose to listen to Him, we will experience restoration. He deserves more from us than we've been giving. He is a good and loving God. His temple has been desolate for far too long.

HIGHER GROUND

I'm pressing on the upward way,
New heights I'm gaining every day;
Still praying as I'm onward bound,
"Lord, plant my feet on higher ground."

Refrain

Lord, lift me up and let me stand,
By faith, on Heaven's table land,
A higher plane than I have found;
Lord, plant my feet on higher ground.

My heart has no desire to stay
Where doubts arise and fears dismay;
Though some may dwell where those abound,
My prayer, my aim, is higher ground.

Refrain

I want to live above the world,
Though Satan's darts at me are hurled;
For faith has caught the joyful sound,
The song of saints on higher ground.

Refrain

I want to scale the utmost height
And catch a gleam of glory bright;
But still I'll pray till Heav'n I've found,
"Lord, plant my feet on higher ground."

Refrain

Written by: Johnson Oatman, Jr.

DAY 2

RETURN

Return: to go back or come back again, to go back in thought, practice or condition, to pass back to an earlier possessor;
Synonym: reciprocate: reciprocate implies a mutual or equivalent exchange or paying back of what one has received.

Yesterday, we read that God's people turned away from Him and defiled His house, causing the desolation to happen. We read how His people refused to listen to His messengers He sent. For the next few days, we will read what these messengers had to say.

Today, we will see for ourselves His reason for allowing the exile and His promises to Israel regarding their restoration. Let's read His promises to Israel spoken through Jeremiah.

Jeremiah 29:1, 10-14

¹ Now these are the words of the letter which Jeremiah the prophet sent from Jerusalem to the rest of the elders of the exile, the priests, the prophets and all the people whom Nebuchadnezzar had taken into exile from Jerusalem to Babylon.

¹⁰ "For thus says the LORD, 'When seventy years have been completed for Babylon, I will visit you and fulfill My good word to you, to bring you back to this place. ¹¹ For I know the plans that

I have for you,' declares the LORD, 'plans for welfare and not for calamity to give you a future and a hope. **¹²** Then you will call upon Me and come and pray to Me, and I will listen to you. **¹³** You will seek Me and find *Me* when you search for Me with all your heart. **¹⁴** I will be found by you,' declares the LORD, 'and I will restore your fortunes and will gather you from all the nations and from all the places where I have driven you,' declares the LORD, 'and I will bring you back to the place from where I sent you into exile.'

The Lord promised to visit and bring back all those taken from Jerusalem to Babylon, in 70 years. His plan for them was for welfare, not calamity and to give them a future and a hope. He would be their Provider. They would no longer wander through life aimlessly. His plan also included open communication. He knew, after being separated for seventy years, they would call upon and pray to Him. He said "I will listen to you." He assured them they would find Him when they searched for Him with all of their heart.

At the beginning of the exile, King Nebuchadnezzar chose many Israeli youths from his captives to serve in his court. They were taught the literature and language of the Chaldeans (Dan 1:3, 4). Daniel was one of these youths. However, he was determined to worship only the God of Israel. He had the God-given gift to know and interpret dreams. He interpreted the king's dream, and in return was made ruler over the whole province of Babylon (Dan. 2:48). Daniel lived through the seventy-years of captivity and was favored by all three kings who reigned during that time. He was used by God as a prophet. At the end of the captivity, Daniel read Jeremiah's letter. Let's see how he reacted to it.

Daniel 9:1-6

¹ In the first year of Darius the son of Ahasuerus, of Median descent, who was made king over the kingdom of the Chaldeans—

² **in the first year of his reign, I, Daniel, observed in the books the number of the years which was revealed as the word of the LORD to Jeremiah the prophet for the completion of the desolations of Jerusalem, namely, seventy years. ³ So I gave my attention to the Lord God to seek Him by prayer and supplications, with fasting, sackcloth and ashes. ⁴ I prayed to the LORD my God and confessed and said, "Alas, O Lord, the great and awesome God, who keeps His covenant and lovingkindness for those who love Him and keep His commandments, ⁵ we have sinned, committed iniquity, acted wickedly and rebelled, even turning aside from Your commandments and ordinances. ⁶ Moreover, we have not listened to Your servants the prophets, who spoke in Your name to our kings, our princes, our fathers and all the people of the land.**

Daniel found that the exile would end after seventy years. He began to pray and fast, knowing the Lord was great and awesome and always kept His promises. As an act of humility he clothed himself with sackcloth and ashes. He confessed the sins of Israel. He acknowledged that they did not listen to the prophets whom God had sent to prevent the exile from happening. He took upon himself the sin of the entire nation, from the king down to all the people. He left no one out and didn't lessen anyone's responsibility, either.

Daniel 9:17-19

¹⁷ So now, our God, listen to the prayer of Your servant and to his supplications, and for Your sake, O Lord, let Your face shine on Your desolate sanctuary. ¹⁸ O my God, incline Your ear and hear! Open Your eyes and see our desolations and the city which is called by Your name; for we are not presenting our supplications before You on account of any merits of our own, but on account of Your great compassion. ¹⁹ O Lord, hear! O Lord, forgive! O Lord, listen and take action! For Your own sake, O my God, do not delay, because Your city and Your people are called by Your name."

We know Daniel has a personal relationship with God, because he expects Him to: listen to his prayers, see the people's predicament, forgive their sin, and help them. He says, "Take action!" Why? For His name sake, since they are called by His name. He is pleading with God to be merciful and to fulfill His Word which He spoke through Jeremiah. He is begging God to restore Jerusalem and Israel.

Daniel took upon himself the sin of the nation. On the cross, Jesus took upon Himself the sin of the world once and for all. Because of this we can boldly come before God in prayer and confess our sin and be forgiven. When we find ourselves in a place of desolation we too would be wise to stop what we were doing and start praying. Praying for the Lord to reveal all that is hindering us from being all He designed us to be. Acknowledging the sin in our lives and asking the Lord to forgive us.

Throughout the Bible, we see Israel and Jerusalem set apart from the rest of the world for God's glory. The Lord desired more than anything to be their All in All. It was and still is about a personal relationship with His people, who are called by His name. He wanted to be known by and through them. He was willing to let them go for seventy years in order to once again have them whole-heartedly for Himself. This is why He allowed the exile. He knew this separation would make them realize how much they really needed Him for guidance and help in everyday life. This passage clearly reveals the Father's heart and how He desired to be a part of their lives on a daily basis.

Israel became a nation again in 1948. Since then, the Lord has been gathering the Jews from the nations and other places where He drove them. He is bringing them back to Israel and Jerusalem, their Promised Land. He is restoring their fortunes. He will never allow them to be removed from the Promised Land again. This is prophecy being fulfilled right before our very eyes.

These plans pertain just as much to us as they do to Israel. Through Jesus, we have been adopted into the family of God. We are joint heirs with Jesus. And all that was given to Jesus while He walked on the earth is now available to us.

The Lord created us for a relationship with Him. He wants to be our best Friend. He wants us to include Him in every decision we make. If we return to Him, He promises to help us.

We've read the Lord's promise to bring Israel back to Jerusalem. We heard Daniel begging the Lord to hear, forgive, and listen to them and to take action on their behalf. We're going to go ahead of our story in order to hear what a couple other prophets of the time had to say to Israel. Many of the captives returned to Jerusalem to rebuild the Temple. The Lord did listen to their petitions and took action on their behalf. However, after they had laid the foundation, the work stopped due to opposition. We'll now read what the Lord said to them in order to spur them on to return and complete the work they had begun.

Haggai 1:2

² "Thus says the LORD of hosts, 'This people says, "The time has not come, *even* the time for the house of the LORD to be rebuilt."'"

God revealed to them that He hears their every word. He knows they decided for themselves that the time was not right to rebuild His house. God knew exactly what they needed to hear in order to get their lives back on the right path. I'm sure everyone who had ever said those words was convicted by them.

He continues to speak:

Haggai 1:4

⁴ "Is it time for you yourselves to dwell in your paneled houses while this house *lies* desolate?"

God asks them this question for several reasons. The first is to make them think about where their hearts are. The second is to let them know that He knows where they live and that they put their own houses before His. He is also reminding them that He is with them and always has been.

Haggai 1:5-7

⁵ Now therefore, thus says the LORD of hosts, "Consider your ways! ⁶ You have sown much, but harvest little; *you* eat, but *there is* not *enough* to be satisfied; *you* drink, but *there is* not *enough* to become drunk; *you* put on clothing, but no one is warm *enough*; and he who earns, earns wages to *put* into a purse with holes."

⁷ Thus says the LORD of hosts, "Consider your ways!

The Lord shouts, "Consider your ways!" He then reveals the effect of putting their houses before His, which is a life of futility and lack. There is no satisfaction or getting ahead. He again shouts, "Consider your ways!"

When we shout at our children, it is because they're not listening or can't hear us when we are speaking calmly. Here the Lord is shouting at Israel: "Consider your ways!" He had great plans for them and couldn't stand to watch them strive any longer. He was determined to get their attention. It was the right time to rebuild the Temple.

Many of us have been blessed because of the faithfulness of our forefathers. We rode in on their shirt-tails, so to speak. Unfortunately, we focused on the effect, which was the blessings, rather than the cause, which was their faithfulness to God through keeping His commandments. Because of this, we see the blessings slowly but surely disappearing and being replaced with futility.

All good things come from God. We should protect our

blessings and take back what has been taken from us. This is a worthy fight. The first step is going back to church and restoring our relationship with our Heavenly Father. Keep in mind that Satan, God's enemy, is fully aware of His ways. He has determined to keep us away from God's house, because he knows that is where we learn how to live a victorious life.

Today, there are lots of people thinking about going back to church. However, most have decided for themselves that the timing isn't right. Most are putting their own houses before God's.

I gave my life back to the Lord in 1994. I was extremely grateful to Him for His grace and mercy toward me. I knew I had overstepped my boundaries and wasn't worthy of His loving kindness. I was overwhelmed by His compassion and love that He demonstrated to me, and was determined to live the rest of my life in a manner that was pleasing to Him. However, I became discouraged. The more I went to church and heard the Word of God spoken, the more I realized how deceived I was. I felt empty and desolate. I needed to find the truth for myself, according to the Bible. So I dove into the scriptures for the answers. As I read the book of Ezra, He spoke to me. He promised to fully restore every area of my life if I would obey Him by doing what He revealed to me. Throughout this book, I will be showing you some of the things He revealed to me that continue to help me along my journey.

Life without satisfaction can clearly be seen today throughout the world. Regardless of what or who we put before God, the result is the same: No satisfaction. That is because our striving is against all that Jesus taught while He lived here on earth.

Jesus said:

Matthew 6:33-34

³³ But seek first His kingdom and His righteousness, and all these

things will be added to you.

³⁴ "So do not worry about tomorrow; for tomorrow will care for itself. Each day has enough trouble of its own.

This is the key to life: Seek first His kingdom and His righteousness then all these things will be added to you.

In the second chapter of Ezra, there is an extensive list of the names and numbers of those who returned to Jerusalem to rebuild the Temple. The Lord noticed them and knew each and every one of them by name. When Jesus returns as King of Kings and Lord of Lords, there will be another roll call. Will your name be on it? Will you be counted in the number?

When we choose to give our lives to Jesus, we become Christians, called by His name. We are His people. This is not on account of our own merit, but because of what He did for us. He chose to die so we can be forgiven. He rose from the dead so we can have eternal life and resurrection power.

However, He cannot bless us individually or as a people if we continue to turn from Him and His commandments. Let's see where His judgment will begin.

I Peter 4:17

¹⁷ For it is time for judgment to begin with the household of God; and if it begins with us first, what will be the outcome for those who do not obey the gospel of God?

How can God bless anyone, if His church, the body of Christ, is not living according to His Word? We are to be the light in the world. Unfortunately, most of what the world has heard regarding the church has not been all that good. There has been way too much sin in the house of the Lord. His judgment has to start here. However, there is hope. It starts with a humble heart.

II Chronicles 7:14

¹⁴ and My people who are called by My name humble themselves and pray and seek My face and turn from their wicked ways, then I will hear from heaven, will forgive their sin and will heal their land.

Humility is a good thing. It reveals our need for the Lord. The Father is here and is willing to forgive and restore us to a right relationship with Him.

There are a lot of good churches. They belong to God. We are His people. It is time for us to start filling them up with our praises. Once we take our rightful place in the church, it will cleanse itself. Don't allow anything or anyone to keep you from God's best any longer.

It is time to return. Return and see that the Lord is good! "Return, O' wanderer, return," the Father says "Return."

Return, O Wanderer, Return

Return, O wanderer, return,
And seek an injured Father's face;
Those warm desires that in thee burn
Were kindled by reclaiming grace.

Return, O wanderer, return,
And seek a Father's melting heart,
Whose pitying eyes thy grief discern,
Whose hand can heal Thine inward smart.

Return, O wanderer, return,
He heard thy deep repentant sigh,
He saw thy softened spirit mourn
When no intruding ear was nigh.

Return, O wanderer, return,
Thy Savior bids thy spirit live;
Go to His bleeding feet, and learn
How freely Jesus can forgive.

Return, O wanderer, return,
And wipe away the falling tear;
'Tis God who says, "No longer mourn,"
'Tis mercy's voice invites thee near.

Written by: William B. Collyer

DAY 3

REDEEMED

Redeemed: To buy back;
To free from captivity by payment or ransom;
To free from the consequences of sin;
To clear; To free from accusation or blame;
To give insight to.

We have been redeemed. We are no longer held captive by Satan due to the consequences of our sin. We are free from accusation and blame. The ransom was paid in full. Jesus paid the price.

Today, we are going to see that God redeemed Israel from its captors.

The Promised Land was full of their enemies. The people were scared. God encouraged them by letting them know that He was with them and would protect them.

He said:

Zechariah 1:16

¹⁶ Therefore thus says the LORD, "I will return to Jerusalem with compassion; My house will be built in it," declares the LORD of hosts, "and a measuring line will be stretched over Jerusalem."'

Here, He says He will return with compassion and His house

will be built, not *could* be built.

As I read this, I saw the Lord's hand stretching a measuring line over Jerusalem. It wasn't lifted; it was set as though He were saying, "This is My city." This vision brought with it a sense of protection and well-being to me.

When we choose to return to our rightful place with the Lord, He will reciprocate. He is waiting for you. He desires to strengthen you and give you courage to overcome the problems of the world. He is very aware of the pull temptation has on our lives. While on earth, He endured every temptation, yet was without sin. This is why He is compassionate and forgiving. He is determined to restore you as His temple. He wants to be a covering over you to shield you from harm. When people see you, they will see His hand on you. Being seen by the world through His people is what brings Him glory.

Trust Him. He is the only One who is always trustworthy.

Zechariah 2:13

13 "Be silent, all flesh, before the LORD; for He is aroused from His holy habitation."

He is telling them to silence their fears. He is with them. He is standing over them. He will protect them.

The Bible reveals again and again that when He is aroused, His enemies had better back off. That is because He is about to let the whole world know Who is to be feared.

Considering the turmoil in the world today, I would say it is very probable that the Lord is once again aroused from His holy habitation. Jesus may not be sitting at the right hand of the Father; He may be standing. In any case, we need to silence our fears and trust that He will protect us from our enemies.

Following is the passage describing Zechariah's vision of Joshua standing before the angel of the Lord.

Zechariah 3:1-7, 9c

¹ Then he showed me Joshua the high priest standing before the angel of the LORD, and Satan standing at his right hand to accuse him. ² The LORD said to Satan, "The LORD rebuke you, Satan! Indeed, the LORD who has chosen Jerusalem rebuke you! Is this not a brand plucked from the fire?" ³ Now Joshua was clothed with filthy garments and standing before the angel. ⁴ He spoke and said to those who were standing before him, saying, "Remove the filthy garments from him." Again he said to him, "See, I have taken your iniquity away from you and will clothe you with festal robes." ⁵ Then I said, "Let them put a clean turban on his head." So they put a clean turban on his head and clothed him with garments, while the angel of the LORD was standing by.

⁶ And the angel of the LORD admonished Joshua, saying, ⁷ "Thus says the LORD of hosts, 'If you will walk in My ways and if you will perform My service, then you will also govern My house and also have charge of My courts, and I will grant you free access among these who are standing here.

⁹ᶜ declares the LORD of hosts, 'and I will remove the iniquity of that land in one day.

This is a vivid picture of our Lord's love and forgiveness, versus Satan our accuser. We'll first look at our accuser. His number-one way of keeping God's people from Him and His church is through condemnation. He has determined to convince you that the Lord will not forgive you, nor does He even care about you. Another name for our accuser is the "father of lies." He is a liar who hates people more than anything. Don't allow him to continue to keep you from God's best.

The Holy Spirit convicts us of our sin. The blood of Jesus cleanses us of our sin. God the Father forgives us of our sin. However, Satan will condemn us with our sin. When he does (not *if*, but *when*), throw it back at him. There is no condemnation with Jesus.

You can return to your rightful place with God and become all that you were designed to be. He does care about you and has promised to forgive you the moment you acknowledge and confess your sin. He has a plan for your future. I love how Joshua's filthy garment was exchanged for festal robes. This is a picture of us, the way the Lord sees us once we've been forgiven.

The Lord told Joshua if he walked in His ways and performs His service, he would govern His house, have charge over His courts and free access among the angels (v7.)

Your place with the Lord shouldn't be taken lightly. If you choose to be obedient and follow Him, He will lead you into a great life. With Jesus, all we need is Him. He is the Perfect Master. He holds the future and desires to lead us into a great life. He is looking for mighty men and women who are willing to lay down their agendas and follow Him. He plans to take back what Satan has stolen from us, and wants to use you to do it. We are ready. Our hardships have taught us to persevere when life gets tough. What Satan meant for evil, the Lord will turn to good. The Lord wants some Davids who can take out some Goliaths and Deborahs who can stand up to a fierce army. We are under attack. We need to return and show the world Who our God is!

The passage ends with the Lord stating He will remove the iniquity (sin) of the land in one day, which He did on the cross. However, as we walked away from the Lord, Satan started taking back control of the land, causing it to become a violent and chaotic mess. When those who've walked away return to Him with repentant hearts, the sin of the land will again be forgiven. We need to get it back under God's covering.

Isaiah was a prophet before the exile. He prophesied what would take place during this time and spoke specifically about Cyrus, the king of Persia who overthrew Nebuchadnezzar and the Babylonian Empire. He allowed some of the exiles to go back to Jerusalem to rebuild the Temple.

Isaiah 44:22

22 "I have wiped out your transgressions like a thick cloud
And your sins like a heavy mist.
Return to Me, for I have redeemed you."

This is a picture of God standing beside Israel, stretching out His arm and literally wiping away the people's sin. He removed the thick cloud and mist that impaired their vision, which was separating them from Himself. Then they could see their way back to Him; so He said, "Return to Me." The Lord tells His people they are redeemed. He bought them back from their captor. They are His.

Isaiah 44:23

23 Shout for joy, O heavens, for the LORD has done it!
Shout joyfully, you lower parts of the earth;
Break forth into a shout of joy, you mountains,
O forest, and every tree in it;
For the LORD has redeemed Jacob
And in Israel He shows forth His glory.

Because the Lord redeemed Jacob (Israel), all of creation is shouting with joy. This reveals that creation is affected when God's people are in bondage and rejoices when they are free.

Isaiah 44:24-27

24 Thus says the LORD, your Redeemer, and the one who formed
you from the womb,

> **"I, the LORD, am the maker of all things,**
> **Stretching out the heavens by Myself**
> **And spreading out the earth all alone,**
> **²⁵ Causing the omens of boasters to fail,**
> **Making fools out of diviners,**
> **Causing wise men to draw back**
> **And turning their knowledge into foolishness,**
> **²⁶ Confirming the word of His servant**
> **And performing the purpose of His messengers.**
> ***It is I*** **who says of Jerusalem, 'She shall be inhabited!'**
> **And of the cities of Judah, 'They shall be built.'**
> **And I will raise up her ruins** *again*.
> **²⁷ "***It is I*** **who says to the depth of the sea, 'Be dried up!'**
> **And I will make your rivers dry.**

In this passage, the Lord reveals Himself as their Redeemer and the Creator of all things (v.24). He says He makes fools out of psychics and those who are wise in their own minds (v.25). He confirms and fulfills the words of His prophets. He alone knows the future. He promises that Jerusalem and Judah will be fully restored (v.26). He reminds them that with a word He dried up the Red Sea when they left Egypt and entered the wilderness, and then dried up the Jordan River when they left the wilderness to enter the Promised Land (v.27).

God sent the prophets so Israel would have a promise to hang onto while in captivity for seventy years. We, too, are encouraged when we read and study prophecy, because we see that God was and is faithful to His Word.

He is Faithful and True. He will never leave nor forsake us. Even when we are stuck between our enemies and a sea, He will make a way out for us. Nothing is impossible with God.

Isaiah 44:28

28 "*It is I* who says of Cyrus, '*He is* My shepherd!
And he will perform all My desire.'
And he declares of Jerusalem, 'She will be built,'
And of the temple, 'Your foundation will be laid.'"

Here, we see that God would redeem His people from Babylon through Cyrus. He would use their captor to be His shepherd, to watch over His flock, Israel. Not only that, but He will use him to perform all of His desires. Why? Because He knew Cyrus would be obedient.

The Lord will use anyone He can trust and who has put their trust in Him.

In verses 26 and 28, God declares that Jerusalem will be rebuilt and her foundation will be laid. These are Words of encouragement. They are straight from the throne of grace. He wanted Israel to know He would not forget them during their seventy-year captivity. He promises they will be restored back to their rightful place with Him in Jerusalem and the Temple will be rebuilt from the foundation up. He is reassuring them that He will see this work through to completion.

The world has been held captive by Satan since the fall of mankind in the Garden of Eden. However, God had the plan of redemption. Cyrus was a foreshadower of Jesus, the Good Shepherd. God sent His One and only Son, Jesus, to redeem us from the hands of Satan, His enemy. He loves all people. Through redemption, we are adopted into His family and are no longer held captive by our sin. He is true to His word and wishes none would perish but all would have eternal life.

Let's listen to Jesus as He talks to Nicodemus a very well-known and respected Pharisee (a rabbi).

John 3:1-3

¹ Now there was a Pharisee, a man named Nicodemus who was a member of the Jewish ruling council. ² He came to Jesus at night and said, "Rabbi, we know that you are a teacher who has come from God. For no one could perform the signs you are doing if God were not with him."

³ Jesus replied, "Very truly I tell you, no one can see the kingdom of God unless they are born again."

This is where the term "born again" is found. It is not church doctrine; it came from the mouth of Jesus Himself. It is to be taken seriously, for it is the only way we will ever see the kingdom of God. When we are born again, we receive the Holy Spirit who gives us insight by opening our eyes to see the kingdom of God.

John 3:4-6

⁴ Nicodemus *said to Him, "How can a man be born when he is old? He cannot enter a second time into his mother's womb and be born, can he?" ⁵ Jesus answered, "Truly, truly, I say to you, unless one is born of water and the Spirit he cannot enter into the kingdom of God. ⁶ That which is born of the flesh is flesh, and that which is born of the Spirit is spirit.

Being born of water speaks of the water in our mother's womb, our first birth, born of the flesh. Born of the Spirit speaks of the indwelling Holy Spirit who enters us and brings us new life. Then we are born again and can be certain that when we pass from this life to the next, our spirit will go directly to heaven, for all eternity. We become spiritual beings.

Jesus continues to talk to Nicodemus by saying:

John 3:16-17

¹⁶ "For God so loved the world, that He gave His only begotten Son, that whoever believes in Him shall not perish, but have eternal life. ¹⁷ For God did not send the Son into the world to judge the world, but that the world might be saved through Him.

Jesus redeemed us when He ransomed His life for us on the cross. By doing so, He traded places with us. He gave His life so we could have eternal life. His blood destroyed the curse that was put on mankind in the Garden of Eden. This means Satan no longer has dominion over us. Jesus was the final blood sacrifice. He is the Lamb of God who takes away the sin of the world.

Let me share with you a vision I had at a Good Friday service, as I was looking at Jesus hanging in agony on the cross. There was a tornado spinning at full speed above Jesus' right side with the tail entering Him. I could see the debris in the tornado. It was the sin of the world. Every sin, past, present and future, was entering Him. He was literally taking upon Himself the sin of the world. The speed and force of entry was horrific. It was as if Jesus would burst. The beatings and scourging He had received before the cross were nothing in comparison to this pain. I saw Adolf Hitler and other evil people in the debris. This is when the Father had to look away, since He cannot look upon sin. Then I saw myself at the foot of the cross. I was committing what I believed to be my worst sin. Jesus looked down from the cross and looked me straight in the eyes letting me know my sin was one of the reasons He chose to die on the cross, and that I was forgiven.

I assure you, your sins were in that violent tornado, as well. He loves you so much that He chose to die for you. Redemption is a personal choice and is available to all who accept what Jesus did for them on the cross. This is done by acknowledging that you are a sinner in need of a Savior and asking Him to forgive and cleanse you from all unrighteousness. Ask Him to come into your heart and abide with you forever. Receive the Holy Spirit with an open heart. You are redeemed.

He Died for Me

I saw One hanging on a tree,
In agony and blood;
He fixed His loving eyes on me,
As near His cross I stood.

Refrain

O, can it be, upon a tree
The Savior died for me?
My soul is thrilled, my heart is filled,
To think He died for me!

Sure, never till my latest breath,
Can I forget that look;
It seemed to charge me with His death,
Though not a word He spoke.

Refrain

My conscience felt and owned the guilt,
And plunged me in despair;
I saw my sins His blood had spilt
And helped to nail Him there.

Refrain

A second look He gave, which said,
"I freely all forgive:
This blood is for your ransom paid,
I die that you may live."

Refrain

Written By: John Newton

DAY 4

CHOSEN

Chosen: one who is the object
of choice or divine favor;
Choose: to select freely
and after consideration.

To be chosen, handpicked by someone is an honor. Being chosen gives you the confidence you need to succeed. It removes some of the doubts that will arise within us.

Remember, before the exile Isaiah foretold of Cyrus' reign and call. Let's hear what the Lord said to Cyrus.

Isaiah 45:1-3

¹ Thus says the LORD to Cyrus His anointed,
Whom I have taken by the right hand,
To subdue nations before him
And to loose the loins of kings;
To open doors before him so that gates will not be shut:

² "I will go before you and make the rough places smooth;
I will shatter the doors of bronze and cut through their iron bars.

³ "I will give you the treasures of darkness

And hidden wealth of secret places,
So that you may know that it is I,
The LORD, the God of Israel, who calls you by your name.

The Lord begins by reassuring Cyrus that He has anointed him. He gave him the divine ability, power and authority to do all that He called him to do. He lets him know that it is He who holds his right hand. He is with him and will remain with him. Why? To subdue nations, break the legs of kings and open doors before him, so that gates will not be shut. He is giving him power over all of his adversaries. No one will keep him from doing what the Lord called him to do. He reassures him that He has smoothed out all the rough places. He promises to supply all his needs through the treasures of darkness (wickedness) and hidden wealth of secret places. God lets Cyrus know He is going to do these things, so he will know beyond a shadow of a doubt that it is He, The Lord, the God of Israel, who calls him by name. The glory belongs to the Lord.

This is a beautiful picture of the Lord reassuring Cyrus of his call and the blessings that come by being chosen of God and in His perfect will. This is true for us today, as well. When we obey God, our needs will be met. He will give us the protection, power and finances needed to do all that He has called us to do. He desires to take us by the right hand and walk with us all the days of our lives.

Let's see why God chose King Cyrus.

Isaiah 45:4-6

⁴ **"For the sake of Jacob My servant,**
　　And Israel My chosen one,
　　I have also called you by your name;
　　I have given you a title of honor
　　Though you have not known Me.

⁵ **"I am the LORD, and there is no other;**

Besides Me there is no God
I will gird you, though you have not known Me;

6 That men may know from the rising to the setting of the sun
That there is no one besides Me.
I am the LORD, and there is no other,

Whenever a sentence starts with the word *for* or *so*, you can, in your mind, put the word *why* in front of it. Here the Lord is telling Cyrus why He called him by name. It was for the sake of Jacob, His servant and Israel, His chosen one. Jacob's name was changed to Israel by God; they are one and the same. King Cyrus' call in life was all for the sake of God's chosen people, Israel. Israel had been subdued for seventy years. Now their God is about to let the world know they are His chosen people. The Lord lets King Cyrus know it was He who gave him a title of honor, King of Persia, even though he didn't know Him.

He is revealing Himself to King Cyrus as the One and only God. He then promises to gird (strengthen) him and again says, "Even though you have not known Me." He wants Cyrus to remember that the only reason he will be able to do the things he is about to do is because He chose him. In other words, it has nothing to do with him. This is a God thing. He explains the reason in the following way: "That men may know from the rising to the setting of the sun that there is no one besides Me. I am the Lord, and there is no other." Cyrus is to give the glory to God, for all men to see and acknowledge there is but one God and He is the God of Israel.

Today, we would also be wise to keep in mind that our successes come from the Lord. We should give Him the glory for every blessing we receive. More often than not, we don't even realize the depth that the Lord is using us for His glory. He told King Cyrus it is for the sake of Israel, not him. However, Cyrus did receive a title of honor and wealth along the way.

Then, the Lord says:

Isaiah 45:8

⁸ "Drip down, O heavens, from above,
　　And let the clouds pour down righteousness;
　　Let the earth open up and salvation bear fruit,
　　And righteousness spring up with it.
　　I, the LORD, have created it.

Evil held God's people down for long enough. He is now calling righteousness to come down from the heavens and be poured out upon Israel. This is a spiritual rain, and rain represents blessings. He is saying, "Receive my blessings and go forth and let your salvation bear fruit; be a witness to the world by living righteously and glorifying Me." He is also speaking to the land. Remember, it was enjoying seventy years of rest. It is now time for the land to start producing fruit for God's people, for they are coming home.

Isaiah 45:9

⁹ "Woe to the one who quarrels with his Maker--
　　An earthenware vessel among the vessels of earth!
　　Will the clay say to the potter, 'What are you doing?'
　　Or the thing you are making say, 'He has no hands'?

Remember that He spoke through Jeremiah, saying, "After seventy years they will desire to be with Me." This is the righteousness now being rained down upon them. Israel is the nation among the nations of earth. They were fighting with their Maker, because they didn't understand why He had to do the things He did.

Isaiah continues to prophesy regarding Cyrus, saying:

Isaiah 45:11-13

¹¹ Thus says the LORD, the Holy One of Israel, and his Maker:

> "Ask Me about the things to come concerning My sons,
> And you shall commit to Me the work of My hands.

¹² "It is I who made the earth, and created man upon it
I stretched out the heavens with My hands
And I ordained all their host.

¹³ "I have aroused him in righteousness
And I will make all his ways smooth;
He will build My city and will let My exiles go free,
Without any payment or reward," says the LORD of hosts.

The Lord wants to hear from King Cyrus. He tells him to ask Him about the things to come concerning Israel's future. By doing so, he is committing their future to Him. He reminds Cyrus that it is He, the Maker of heaven and earth, who is in control of all things. He then says Cyrus will build His city and will release Israel from captivity at no cost. In others words, He is telling Cyrus that he will do this for free. Your reward will come from Me, not Israel. The Lord is encouraging Cyrus by letting him know that He is with him and will make sure he is successful. His path will be made smooth.

The Lord will help you get to this point in life, as well. Cyrus respected and had a holy fear of the Lord. This is also what He wants from us. Then, He can use us to our fullest potential. He wants us to commit our future to Him. There is no end to the peace that comes to a life committed to the Lord. There is peace even in the roughest situations, because we know the Lord will make our way smooth. Everything will work together for the good, because we love Him and are called according to His purpose (Romans 8:28).

Isaiah continues to prophesy regarding Israel's salvation and future.

Isaiah 45:17

¹⁷ Israel has been saved by the LORD

With an everlasting salvation;
You will not be put to shame or humiliated
To all eternity.

This is futuristic, because we know Israel has been shamed and humiliated by their enemies since the time this was spoken. The Lord is promising them that this is only temporary. A day is coming when they will be victorious and the whole world will see it. They have been saved with an everlasting salvation. These words have encouraged Israel for thousands of years, and continue to do so.

God chose Cyrus to rebuild Israel and Jerusalem for the sake of Israel, His chosen people. Now we'll see whom He chose to be holy and blameless. Paul, the Pharisee of Pharisees, who became a believer, wrote the following passage to the church in Ephesus (Eph. 1:1):

Ephesians 1:3-5

³ Blessed be the God and Father of our Lord Jesus Christ, who has blessed us with every spiritual blessing in the heavenly places in Christ, ⁴ just as He chose us in Him before the foundation of the world, that we would be holy and blameless before Him in love. ⁵ He predestined us to adoption as sons through Jesus Christ to Himself, according to the kind intention of His will,

By choosing to die for us, Jesus made a way for us to be adopted into the family of God. God chose us before the foundation of the world to be holy and blameless before Him in love. He is with us and has enabled us to live holy and blameless lives by blessing us with every spiritual blessing in heaven. We are not powerless. All of His power is available to us. All we need to do is call upon the name of Jesus.

Once we accept Jesus as our Lord and Savior and choose to follow Him, we will receive the blessings. Then our salvation will bear fruit, and it will make a difference. We will become world changers. Our lives will be of great purpose. He plans to show the world through you, from the rising to the setting of the sun, that there is no one besides Him. He is the Lord, and there is no other!

We are coming into a time in history where there will be great signs and wonders. Miracles will be expected by those who believe in Him. These will be done through His obedient children. He will pour out His Spirit upon us and we will have power from on high. There will be no end to the things we see in these latter years (John 14:12-15).

Since we have been adopted into His family through Jesus, we can now claim all of these passages for ourselves. He desires to prove Himself to us as the Holy One of Israel, the maker of heaven and earth. He said, "And you shall commit to Me the work of My hands." When we ask Him about our future we are at the same time committing it to Him. It goes something like this: "Lord, You know the future, You know what's coming my way; reveal it to me so I can do what I can to prepare for it." He will bless everything we commit to Him.

God allows the things of the world to break us, in order to draw us back to Himself. The heavens are open and they are pouring down righteousness upon the peoples of the world, because they are open to hear and receive the good news. Salvation will bear her fruit and God will be glorified through His chosen servants. He has anointed His servants whom He has called by name to subdue nations. He is opening doors that have been closed. He is making the rough places smooth.

You are His chosen vessel. He has called you by name. Take time to look at your life and all that He has given you. Are you doing what He has asked of you? Are you the best spouse you can be? Are you the best employee you can be? How are you as a parent? The Bible says to him who is faithful with little, much will be given. Many are called, but few are chosen. Determine to live a life worthy of your call and He will choose to use you in ways you never dreamed possible. Come and see that the Lord is good.

A Mighty Fortress Is Our God

A mighty fortress is our God, a bulwark never failing;
Our helper He, amid the flood of mortal ills prevailing:
For still our ancient foe doth seek to work us woe;
His craft and power are great, and, armed with cruel hate,
On earth is not his equal.

Did we in our own strength confide, our striving would be losing;
Were not the right Man on our side, the Man of God's own choosing:
Dost ask who that may be? Christ Jesus, it is He;
Lord Sabaoth, His Name, from age to age the same,
And He must win the battle.

And though this world, with devils filled, should threaten to undo us,
We will not fear, for God hath willed His truth to triumph through us:
The Prince of Darkness grim, we tremble not for him;
His rage we can endure, for lo, his doom is sure,
One little word shall fell him.

That word above all earthly powers, no thanks to them, abideth;
The Spirit and the gifts are ours through Him Who with us sideth:
Let goods and kindred go, this mortal life also;
The body they may kill: God's truth abideth still,
His kingdom is forever.

Written by: Martin Luther
Translated by: Frederick H. Hedge

DAY 5

FAVOR

Favor: friendly regard shown to another, especially by a superior; approving consideration or attention. Attention: sympathetic consideration of the needs and wants of others.

Today, we begin our journey of restoration through the book of Ezra.

Ezra 1:1-5

¹ Now in the first year of Cyrus king of Persia, in order to fulfill the word of the LORD by the mouth of Jeremiah, the LORD stirred up the spirit of Cyrus king of Persia, so that he sent a proclamation throughout all his kingdom, and also *put it* in writing, saying:

² "Thus says Cyrus king of Persia, 'The LORD, the God of heaven, has given me all the kingdoms of the earth and He has appointed me to build Him a house in Jerusalem, which is in Judah. ³ Whoever there is among you of all His people, may his God be with him! Let him go up to Jerusalem which is in Judah and rebuild the house of the LORD, the God of Israel; He is the God who is in Jerusalem. ⁴ Every survivor, at whatever place he may live, let the men of that place support him with silver and gold, with goods and cattle, together with a freewill offering for the house of God which is in Jerusalem.'"

⁵ Then the heads of fathers' *households* of Judah and Benjamin and the priests and the Levites arose, even everyone whose spirit God had stirred to go up and rebuild the house of the LORD which is in Jerusalem.

God is faithful. Here we clearly see the fulfillment of the prophetic word of Isaiah regarding Cyrus. Remember Cyrus was not even king when Isaiah spoke these words: Nebuchadnezzar was king. Cyrus knew that he owed everything he had to the God of Israel. He was unashamed; he proclaimed it throughout his kingdom and also put it in writing. He proclaimed liberty to all of God's people. They were told to go up out of captivity into Jerusalem to rebuild the house of the Lord. Cyrus also called every survivor to support the building with silver, gold, goods and cattle. He knew they would need resources of supplies and food to eat during their time of rebuilding.

Most of today's leaders are more concerned about pleasing people rather than God. Therefore, we see strong nations becoming weaker and weaker. There is a saying: "Those who won't stand for anything will fall for everything." We need to take back our nations for God, one person at a time. It is time to come back and partake of the Lord's favor.

This scripture says everyone whose spirit God had stirred to go up and rebuild the house of the Lord arose. I say arise and determine to rebuild your temple with the ways of the Lord. There are areas in our lives in which we need favor by those in authority over us in order to move forward in God's plan. Ask Him to give you favor. He will. He gave the Israelites favor through their captor, the least likely person they expected to receive help from. Proverbs 21:1 says, "The king's heart is like channels of water in the hand of the LORD; He turns it wherever He wishes." This passage clearly shows Him doing just that. Cyrus was the king of Persia, the Israelites were his captives, but he let them go. Expect the Lord to move the hearts of those who hold you captive. He is able. Pray for favor.

Ezra 3:1-3

¹ Now when the seventh month came, and the sons of Israel were in the cities, the people gathered together as one man to Jerusalem. ² Then Jeshua the son of Jozadak and his brothers the priests, and Zerubbabel the son of Shealtiel and his brothers arose and built the altar of the God of Israel to offer burnt offerings on it, as it is written in the law of Moses, the man of God. ³ So they set up the altar on its foundation, for they were terrified because of the peoples of the lands; and they offered burnt offerings on it to the LORD, burnt offerings morning and evening.

Here, we see the Israelites back in Jerusalem in the seventh month for the feast. This is the first time in seventy years they've been able to do so. Jeshua is also known as Joshua. He is Joshua, the high priest, spoken of in Zechariah's vision. Those living in the surrounding area near the temple are those who moved in when the Israelites were taken out into captivity. These people were not glad to see them return, regardless of the king's proclamation. They knew it was only a matter of time before the Israelites would take back their land. For their part, the Israelites were terrified, but they came back anyway, putting their faith in their God. They sought His favor through burnt offerings, and He was faithful.

He still is faithful and He always will be. We can count on Him just as the Israelites did. Step out in faith and please the One who favors you. Don't be a people-pleaser, allowing what others might say or think to keep you from making a stand. It takes boldness to unashamedly show the world Who your God is. Become the leader you wish others were. Allow God's favor to fall upon you in every area of your life.

Let's see why God showed Israel such great favor and how the

Word of Ezra is being fulfilled before our own eyes. We will read about this in the book of Ezekiel, who was another prophet during the exile.

Ezekiel 36:22-23

²² "Therefore say to the house of Israel, 'Thus says the Lord GOD, "It is not for your sake, O house of Israel, that I am about to act, but for My holy name, which you have profaned among the nations where you went. ²³ I will vindicate the holiness of My great name which has been profaned among the nations, which you have profaned in their midst. Then the nations will know that I am the LORD," declares the Lord GOD, "when I prove Myself holy among you in their sight.

We read earlier how God chose Cyrus to restore Israel and Jerusalem for Israel's sake. Now, we read how God chose to favor Israel for His sake, not theirs. Israel did nothing to receive God's favor. The only thing that makes them different from anyone else is Him. He alone is holy. He chose to reveal His holiness to the nations through them.

Ezekiel 36:24

²⁴ For I will take you from the nations, gather you from all the lands and bring you into your own land.

He then tells Israel everything He is going to do for them. He's going to take them from the nations and bring them to their own land. We've seen this with our own eyes. They are still returning to Israel from other nations.

Ezekiel 36:25-27

²⁵ Then I will sprinkle clean water on you, and you will be clean; I will cleanse you from all your filthiness and from all your idols. ²⁶ Moreover, I will give you a new heart and put a new spirit within

you; and I will remove the heart of stone from your flesh and give you a heart of flesh. **²⁷ I will put My Spirit within you and cause you to walk in My statutes, and you will be careful to observe My ordinances.**

This is the promise of redemption, being cleansed from our sin, and given a new heart and the indwelling Spirit. He says the Holy Spirit will cause you to walk in "My statutes and observe My ordinances." He promises to save them from their uncleanness, which is sin.

We saw this promise fulfilled on the cross. The blood of Jesus is the only thing that cleanses us of sin. Through Jesus, we are saved. He is the promised Savior of Israel and the world. The twelve disciples and those in the early church were all Jews. A day is coming when we will see the nation of Israel's eyes open to the gospel message.

Ezekiel 36:28

²⁸ You will live in the land that I gave to your forefathers; so you will be My people, and I will be your God.

Clearly, the Lord states they will live in the land of their forefathers and be His people, and He will be their God. Don't forget that the reason is to vindicate the holiness of His great name (v. 23).

Ezekiel 36:29-30

²⁹ Moreover, I will save you from all your uncleanness; and I will call for the grain and multiply it, and I will not bring a famine on you. 30 I will multiply the fruit of the tree and the produce of the field, so that you will not receive again the disgrace of famine among the nations.

After salvation, He promises to multiply the fruit of the tree and produce of the field. Why? So they will not receive again the disgrace of famine among the nations. This day is here, and we will see many come to Christ. He is faithful and true.

Ezekiel 36:31-32

³¹ Then you will remember your evil ways and your deeds that were not good, and you will loathe yourselves in your own sight for your iniquities and your abominations. ³² I am not doing *this* for your sake," declares the Lord GOD, "let it be known to you. Be ashamed and confounded for your ways, O house of Israel!"

Then they will see their sin and the sin of their forefathers. They will remember their evil ways and their deeds that were not good, as we saw with Daniel when he read Jeremiah's letter. However, they will at the same time be overwhelmed with joy for the grace and mercy of God. They will one day rule with Jesus; this is favor!

The Lord is ready to vindicate the holiness of His great name which has been profaned among the nations, which we have profaned in their midst. When He proves Himself faithful among us in the sight of the nations, they will know that He is the Lord. We, too, profaned His name. His decision to choose us has nothing to do with anything we've ever done. It's all about Him and His love for all people. He wishes none would perish. All we have to do is give our lives to Him and He will cleanse us of our sin. He promises to give us a new heart and put His Spirit within us, removing our heart of stone and replacing it with one of flesh. His Spirit within us enables us to walk in His ways.

Know that the Lord plans to restore you to your rightful place. He will care for all of your daily needs. Repent and be ashamed of your former ways. This should be a time of humility. We should be disgusted with ourselves and the way we chose to abandon the One who loves us, the Creator of heaven and earth. Be thankful for His mercies, for they are new every morning.

King Solomon wrote:

Proverbs 14:35

[35] The king's favor is toward a servant who acts wisely, But his anger is toward him who acts shamefully.

King Cyrus was favored because the Lord knew he would give Him the glory before the entire world. Be wise in your actions and give God the glory, then you will be favored by the King of Kings.

O Jesus I Have Promised

O Jesus, I have promised to serve Thee to the end;
Be Thou forever near me, my Master and my Friend;
I shall not fear the battle if Thou art by my side,
Nor wander from the pathway if Thou wilt be my Guide.

O let me feel Thee near me! The world is ever near;
I see the sights that dazzle, the tempting sounds I hear;
My foes are ever near me, around me and within;
But Jesus, draw Thou nearer, and shield my soul from sin.

O let me hear Thee speaking in accents clear and still,
Above the storms of passion, the murmurs of self will.
O speak to reassure me, to hasten or control;
O speak, and make me listen, Thou Guardian of my soul.

O Jesus, Thou hast promised to all who follow Thee
That where Thou art in glory there shall Thy servant be.
And Jesus, I have promised to serve Thee to the end;
O give me grace to follow, my Master and my Friend.

O let me see Thy footprints, and in them plant mine own;
My hope to follow duly is in Thy strength alone.
O guide me, call me, draw me, uphold me to the end;
And then in Heaven receive me, my Savior and my Friend.

Written by: John E. Bode

DAY 6

FOUNDATION

Foundation: a basis (as a tenet, principle or axiom) upon which something stands or is supported; an understanding base or support; especially the whole masonry structure of a building. Found: to take the first steps in building; to establish (as an institution), often with provision for future maintenance.

Today, we will lay the foundation of our restoration.

Ezra 3:8-9

⁸ Now in the second year of their coming to the house of God at Jerusalem in the second month, Zerubbabel the son of Shealtiel and Jeshua the son of Jozadak and the rest of their brothers the priests and the Levites, and all who came from the captivity to Jerusalem, began *the* work and appointed the Levites from twenty years and older to oversee the work of the house of the LORD. ⁹ Then Jeshua *with* his sons and brothers stood united *with* Kadmiel and his sons, the sons of Judah *and* the sons of Henadad *with* their sons and brothers the Levites, to oversee the workmen in the temple of God.

Two years have passed, the plans to rebuild the temple have been prepared, the workers and overseers have been carefully chosen and there is unity. It is time to rebuild the temple and it must start with the foundation.

While I read about the foundation of the Temple in the book of Ezra, I realized my foundation was weak at best. Being in construction, I was aware that the depth of the foundation determined the potential height of the building. I wanted a deep foundation that I could build my new life upon. I realized I wasted a lot of years and was determined to make up for lost time. I knew if I had a shallow foundation, I would surely fall when trouble came my way. Therefore, I studied the Bible every chance I could. I wanted everyone to know that I could and would stand for Jesus, in every circumstance in which I found myself.

Following is perhaps the most well-known passage on building a strong foundation. These are the last words Jesus spoke in the Sermon on the Mount (Matt. 5-7:27).

Matthew 7:24-27

24 "Therefore everyone who hears these words of Mine and acts on them, may be compared to a wise man who built his house on the rock. 25 And the rain fell, and the floods came, and the winds blew and slammed against that house; and yet it did not fall, for it had been founded on the rock. 26 Everyone who hears these words of Mine and does not act on them, will be like a foolish man who built his house on the sand. 27 The rain fell, and the floods came, and the winds blew and slammed against that house; and it fell—and great was its fall."

In the Sermon on the Mount, Jesus taught the large crowd that had followed Him how to live a life that is pleasing to the Father. He said we will be compared to a wise man who built his house on a rock, *if* we live our lives according to His Words in the Sermon on the Mount. *Then*, when adversity comes our way we will not fall, because we are founded on the rock. Jesus is the rock; all other ground is sinking sand.

Matthew 7:28-29

²⁸ When Jesus had finished these words, the crowds were amazed at His teaching; ²⁹ for He was teaching them as *one* **having authority, and not as their scribes.**

Let's see what John, Jesus' beloved disciple, said about Him.

John 1:1-5, 14

¹ In the beginning was the Word, and the Word was with God, and the Word was God. ² He was in the beginning with God. ³ All things came into being through Him, and apart from Him nothing came into being that has come into being. ⁴ In Him was life, and the life was the Light of men. ⁵ The Light shines in the darkness, and the darkness did not comprehend it.

¹⁴ And the Word became flesh, and dwelt among us, and we saw His glory, glory as of the only begotten from the Father, full of grace and truth.

John is describing Jesus and calls Him the Word. He tells us Jesus was not only with God at the time of creation, but was God, and all things were created through Him. In Him was life, the Light of Men; the Word became flesh and dwelt among us, full of grace and truth.

Jesus is the infallible Word of God. The Bible is the revelation of Jesus from beginning to end. He is on every single page.

Let's see what the apostle Paul had to say about our foundation.

Ephesians 2:19-22

¹⁹ So then you are no longer strangers and aliens, but you are fellow citizens with the saints, and are of God's household, ²⁰ having been built on the foundation of the apostles and prophets, Christ Jesus Himself being the corner *stone*, **²¹ in whom the whole building, being fitted together, is growing into a holy temple in the Lord, ²²**

in whom you also are being built together into a dwelling of God in the Spirit.

Here, Paul is letting us know that when we chose to make Jesus our Lord and Savior, we became part of God's household. This passage describes the church as being made with the saints, as a dwelling place for the Holy Spirit, built on the foundation of the apostles and prophets. Jesus is the corner stone, in whom everything is lined up with and fitted together into a holy temple.

We align ourselves with Jesus by acting according to His Word. This passage calls the prophets and apostles the foundation. Therefore, we need to read and understand their teachings, which are found in the books of the prophets, from Isaiah in the Old Testament throughout the New Testament.

Jesus asked His disciples who they thought He was.

Matthew 16:15-18

15 He *said to them, "But who do you say that I am?" 16 Simon Peter answered, "You are the Christ, the Son of the living God." 17 And Jesus said to him, "Blessed are you, Simon Barjona, because flesh and blood did not reveal *this* to you, but My Father who is in heaven. 18 I also say to you that you are Peter, and upon this rock I will build My church; and the gates of Hades will not overpower it.

Peter was one of His apostles. Jesus tells him that he is the rock that He will build His church on.

God reveals the coming Messiah through Isaiah, the prophet.

Isaiah 9:6, 7

6 For a child will be born to us, a son will be given to us;
And the government will rest on His shoulders;
And His name will be called Wonderful Counselor, Mighty
God, Eternal Father, Prince of Peace.

⁷ There will be no end to the increase of His government or of peace,
   On the throne of David and over his kingdom,
   To establish it and to uphold it with justice and righteousness
   From then on and forevermore
   The zeal of the LORD of hosts will accomplish this.

The coming Messiah will be a baby boy born to Israel and given to Israel. He will be called Wonderful Counselor, Mighty God, Eternal Father and Prince of Peace. These names clearly let us know that He and the Father are One. He will rule His kingdom on the throne of David forever. There will be no end to the increase of His government or of peace. He is describing Jesus and His kingdom. He will govern the church and, as it grows, His government will increase. He will establish and uphold it with justice and righteousness.

It is important for us to know that we are under grace. However, we also need to remember that we are under Jesus' authority and are to live our lives accordingly.

In this passage alone, He is called by five different names. There is power in His names. When we call Him by them, we can expect Him to move in them. One of my favorite names for the Lord is Wonderful Counselor. Therefore, I go to Him for counsel, and I am not deceived by ungodly counsel. Go to Him as Mighty God when it feels like you are being attacked from every side. He will fight your battles. Go to Him as Eternal Father, when you feel like everyone has deserted you. He will always be there for you. When you are going through difficult times, go to Him as your Prince of Peace. He will give you peace in the middle of your storm.

He is the Lord of hosts. He will dispatch His angels to protect and encourage you when needed. Decide to learn His names and begin to call out to Him in faith expecting Him to come to your aid. Lay a deep foundation that you can firmly stand and build your life upon. You are a part of His kingdom. Therefore, you have the right and privilege to call upon Him. He loves you more than you will ever know.

Following is a passage that reveals how we are to live as part of His kingdom.

Colossians 1:9-13

⁹ For this reason also, since the day we heard *of it*, we have not ceased to pray for you and to ask that you may be filled with the knowledge of His will in all spiritual wisdom and understanding, ¹⁰ so that you will walk in a manner worthy of the Lord, to please *Him* in all respects, bearing fruit in every good work and increasing in the knowledge of God; ¹¹ strengthened with all power, according to His glorious might, for the attaining of all steadfastness and patience; joyously ¹² giving thanks to the Father, who has qualified us to share in the inheritance of the saints in Light.

¹³ For He rescued us from the domain of darkness, and transferred us to the kingdom of His beloved Son, ¹⁴ in whom we have redemption, the forgiveness of sins.

We are no longer under Satan's control, in his domain of darkness. We have been transferred to Jesus' kingdom through redemption, the forgiveness of sins. We are to pray continuously for divine wisdom, knowledge and understanding, so we can walk in a manner worthy of the Lord.

The apostle Paul wrote about being firmly rooted and built up in Christ and established in our faith. He says we need to walk in Jesus as we were instructed, overflowing with gratitude.

Colossians 2:6-10

⁶ Therefore as you have received Christ Jesus the Lord, *so* walk in Him, ⁷ having been firmly rooted *and now* being built up in Him and established in your faith, just as you were instructed, *and*

overflowing with gratitude.

⁸ See to it that no one takes you captive through philosophy and empty deception, according to the tradition of men, according to the elementary principles of the world, rather than according to Christ. ⁹ For in Him all the fullness of Deity dwells in bodily form, ¹⁰ and in Him you have been made complete, and He is the head over all rule and authority;

Paul then warns us about those who will come and attempt to take us captive through philosophy and empty deception. In Jesus, the fullness of Deity dwells; He is the head over all rule and authority. In Him, we are made whole.

King David wrote the following Psalm explaining what we need to do in order to be blessed and prosper.

Psalm 1:1-3

¹ How blessed is the man who does not walk
    in the counsel of the wicked,
    Nor stand in the path of sinners,
    Nor sit in the seat of scoffers!

² But his delight is in the law of the LORD,
    And in His law he meditates day and night.

³ He will be like a tree firmly planted by streams of water,
    Which yields its fruit in its season
    And its leaf does not wither;
    And in whatever he does, he prospers.

This passage points out things we should and shouldn't do and the blessings that will follow.

When we seek counsel, it is extremely important to make sure it is from someone who is rooted in the Word of God. We need godly counsel. The last thing we need is more counsel from those who counsel according to the tradition of men or according to the elementary principles of the world, rather than according to Christ. We are not to stand in the paths of sinners, meaning that we are not to be counted as one of them. We are to minister to those the Lord brings onto our path, not the other way around. Yes, Jesus did hang out with sinners. However, they deliberately sought Him out, looking for help and answers. They came onto His path. This passage also says we are not to sit with scoffers. It is important for us to surround ourselves with people who will encourage us in our walk with the Lord, not tear it down.

We are to delight ourselves in the law of the Lord and meditate on it day and night. In other words, we are to line up everything in our lives according to the Word of God. Nothing is to be apart from it. We will then find ourselves rooted and founded in His Word. It will overcome our thinking. Our thinking will be transformed into the mind of Christ.

Then and only then can we expect the blessings that come from those choices. We will be like trees firmly planted by streams of water. Provision for all of our needs will be met. We will receive from the Holy Spirit insight and power for each new day. Our lives will be fruitful in season, they will make a difference. We will be like a leaf that does not wither, having strength for each new day. We will prosper in all that we do.

Delight in the Word of God and meditate on it day and night. Expect the Holy Spirit to lead and guide you. He will give you divine wisdom, knowledge and understanding in all things.

King David wrote:

Psalm 37:4

⁴ Delight yourself in the LORD;
    And He will give you the desires of your heart.

A good way to get to know the Lord is to read five chapters in Psalms and one in Proverbs every day. In doing so, you'll read through both books in a month. Read them according to the day of the month. They will strengthen your foundation and give you guidance for a daily walk that will not fail. Proverbs is full of promises that reveal the "ifs" and "thens" of life. Most promises come with an "if" and a "then." *If* we choose to obey them, *then* we'll receive the promises of the Lord.

When I first read the book of Proverbs, after coming back to the Lord, I was amazed at the truths I found. I quickly realized that I had been living my life on the side of the curses mentioned in Proverbs. As I read, I was remembering things I had done and, sure enough, the results were exactly as it is written. I determined to make note of what I needed to do in order to live on the side of the blessings. I can say for sure that the "ifs" and "thens" of Proverbs are very real and remain true today.

Following is a prayer you can pray for a strong foundation:

Dear Heavenly Father,

Help me build a firm foundation to build my life upon, a foundation based on Your Word, the revelation of Jesus Christ. Teach me Your Word through the Holy Spirit, so it will come to life for me. Let me hear Your voice. Give me divine wisdom, knowledge and understanding. I want Jesus to be the Solid Rock on which I stand.

In Jesus' name I pray,

Amen.

The Bible says:

Isaiah 26:4
4 "Trust in the LORD forever,
For in GOD the LORD, we have an everlasting Rock.

Matthew 5:17-19

[17] "Do not think that I came to abolish the Law or the Prophets; I did not come to abolish but to fulfill. [18] For truly I say to you, until heaven and earth pass away, not the smallest letter or stroke shall pass from the Law until all is accomplished. [19] Whoever then annuls one of the least of these commandments, and teaches others *to do* the same, shall be called least in the kingdom of heaven; but whoever keeps and teaches *them*, he shall be called great in the kingdom of heaven.

Psalm 119:60

[60] I hastened and did not delay
    To keep Your commandments.

We cannot keep or teach the commandments of the Lord if we don't know them. Reading your Bible is a must, if you want to be all that the Lord designed you to be, and if you want Him to restore to you all that the enemy has taken from you and your family. This is His desire.

Jesus suffered great persecution but was without sin. He received His strength from the Word of God. He stood on the promises of the Father. We need to do the same.

Joshua 24:15c

[15c] "as for me and my house, we will serve the LORD."

Choose this day whom you will serve, and determine to lay a deep foundation that will not crumble under the stress of the world. Difficult times will come. However, with Jesus as your firm foundation, you will remain standing through it all.

How Firm a Foundation

How firm a foundation, ye saints of the Lord,
Is laid for your faith in His excellent Word!
What more can He say than to you He hath said,
You, who unto Jesus for refuge have fled?

In every condition, in sickness, in health;
In poverty's vale, or abounding in wealth;
At home and abroad, on the land, on the sea,
As thy days may demand, shall thy strength ever be.

Fear not, I am with thee, O be not dismayed,
For I am thy God and will still give thee aid;
I'll strengthen and help thee, and cause thee to stand
Upheld by My righteous, omnipotent hand.

When through the deep waters I call thee to go,
The rivers of woe shall not thee overflow;
For I will be with thee, thy troubles to bless,
And sanctify to thee thy deepest distress.

When through fiery trials thy pathways shall lie,
My grace, all sufficient, shall be thy supply;
The flame shall not hurt thee; I only design
Thy dross to consume, and thy gold to refine.

Even down to old age all My people shall prove
My sovereign, eternal, unchangeable love;
And when hoary hairs shall their temples adorn,
Like lambs they shall still in My bosom be borne.

The soul that on Jesus has leaned for repose,
I will not, I will not desert to its foes;
That soul, though all hell should endeavor to shake,
I'll never, no never, no never forsake.

Written by: John Rippon
From a selection of Hymns

DAY 7

PRAISE

Praise: an expression of approval: worship;
Worship: worthiness, respect;
reverence offered a divine being or supernatural power;
a form of religious practice with its creed and ritual;
extravagant respect or admiration for or devotion to an
object of esteem (worship of the dollar).

Now that we've made Jesus our foundation, praise is in order.

Ezra 3:10-11

¹⁰ Now when the builders had laid the foundation of the temple of the LORD, the priests stood in their apparel with trumpets, and the Levites, the sons of Asaph, with cymbals, to praise the LORD according to the directions of King David of Israel. ¹¹ They sang, praising and giving thanks to the LORD, *saying*, "For He is good, for His lovingkindness is upon Israel forever." And all the people shouted with a great shout when they praised the LORD because the foundation of the house of the LORD was laid.

The Israelites sang praises to the Lord, once the foundation of the temple was laid. They couldn't help but worship Him. Their lives were finally being restored after seventy years of captivity. They sang, praising and giving thanks to the Lord, for they knew His goodness and loving kindness were upon them and would be forever.

It is important to understand that God is a God of order. There is a reason for everything written in the Bible. The priests stood in their apparel with trumpets and the Levites with cymbals, according to the direction of King David. Even the apparel of the priests was ordained by God, to Moses, in the wilderness. As you read the Bible, you will see that God left us with instructions on how to carry things out and who is to do what. Trumpets shouted victory and cymbals led them into worship.

Praising the Lord is a natural response when we've given our lives to Him. We praise Him because we realize He is with us and will be with us for eternity.

The first commandment is:

Exodus 20:3

³ "You shall have no other gods before Me.

The second commandment is:

Exodus 20:4

⁴ "You shall not make for yourself an idol, or any likeness of what is in heaven above or on the earth beneath or in the water under the earth.

We serve a jealous God, and it is Him and Him alone we are to praise. Today, we see the results that occur when we lose the way and worship something or someone other than God. The worship of money and the things it has to offer have caused many to fall away from the One true God. He will not share His glory with another. He is worthy of all the honor, glory and praise.

The Bible says the Lord inhabits the praises of His people and that all creation praises Him. Following are some verses that speak of creation praising the Lord:

Psalm 89:5

**⁵ The heavens will praise Your wonders, O LORD;
Your faithfulness also in the assembly of the holy ones.**

Psalm 148:3

**³ Praise Him, sun and moon;
Praise Him, all stars of light!**

Psalm 66:4

**⁴ "All the earth will worship You,
And will sing praises to You;
They will sing praises to Your name."
Selah.**

Luke 19:40

⁴⁰ But Jesus answered, "I tell you, if these become silent, the stones will cry out!"

We just read, the heavens, sun, moon and earth praise Him. Jesus said if the people become silent, the stones will cry out!

Following are some examples of the way angels praise Him:

Isaiah was taken up to the throne room of God, where he heard the seraphim praising the Lord.

Isaiah 6:1-3

¹ In the year of King Uzziah's death I saw the Lord sitting on a throne, lofty and exalted, with the train of His robe filling the temple. ² Seraphim stood above Him, each having six wings: with two he covered his face, and with two he covered his feet, and with two he flew. ³ And one called out to another and said, "Holy, Holy,

Holy, is the LORD of hosts, The whole earth is full of His glory."

The multitude of angels that appeared to the shepherds in the field the night Jesus was born praised Him. They sang about Jesus, the Peace that is now among men with whom He is well pleased.

Luke 2:13, 14

13 And suddenly there appeared with the angel a multitude of the heavenly host praising God and saying,

14 "Glory to God in the highest, And on earth peace among men with whom He is pleased."

According to the following scripture, we were made to praise our Creator.

Exodus 15:2

2 "The LORD is my strength and song,
And He has become my salvation;
This is my God, and I will praise Him;
My father's God, and I will extol Him

I gave my life back to the Lord on a Saturday afternoon. I went to a little church in my neighborhood the next morning. When I walked in, the choir was singing a hymn. Because I was so grateful to be back in the house of the Lord, I began to cry and my tears literally poured down my face. The choir saw me crying and they all began to cry. It was something else. There is a passage about a woman who was forgiven so much, that she cried and with her tears she washed the feet of Jesus. I was that woman, on that Sunday morning. After that I began to sing praises to the Lord every chance I had. I couldn't stop singing. I woke up singing. I sang in my car. I sang doing dishes. I went to bed singing. Praising the Lord became a part of who I was.

Jesus said:

John 4:24

²⁴ God is spirit, and those who worship Him must worship in spirit and truth."

When we praise the Lord, it is to be from the heart, in spirit and in truth. This brings us into the spiritual realm. It brings us into the throne room of grace where Isaiah went. This is where Jesus is seated at the right hand of the Father and where we join the angels in their worship. There is now power and healing here for those who dare to enter into His Presence.

We worship the Lord with our praises from our lips, instruments, dance and however else He leads us. True worship is led by Him; we don't conjure it up. It comes to us through the indwelling Holy Spirit. It is something we shouldn't try to contain. It should become a way of life for all believers. When fully surrendered to God, we can wake up with a new song in our hearts daily, because He will lead us in our praise. It is His desire that we live a life of praise and see Him in every situation, trusting He is working things out for us. Therefore, we praise Him and give Him all the glory.

Psalm 63:3

**³ Because Your lovingkindness is better than life,
My lips will praise You.**

Psalm 150:3

**³ Praise Him with trumpet sound;
Praise Him with harp and lyre.**

The lame man, who was healed by Jesus, praised Him.

Acts 3:8

⁸ With a leap he stood upright and *began* to walk; and he entered

the temple with them, walking and leaping and praising God.

II Samuel 6:14

¹⁴ **And David was dancing before the LORD with all** *his* **might, and David was wearing a linen ephod.**

Spirit-led praise is beautiful.

Perhaps the loudest and most joyful praise ever heard was the praise of the people, when Jesus entered Jerusalem for His final Passover Feast.

John 12:12-15

¹² **On the next day the large crowd who had come to the feast, when they heard that Jesus was coming to Jerusalem,** ¹³ **took the branches of the palm trees and went out to meet Him, and** *began* **to shout, "Hosanna! BLESSED IS HE WHO COMES IN THE NAME OF THE LORD, even the King of Israel."** ¹⁴ **Jesus, finding a young donkey, sat on it; as it is written, 15 "FEAR NOT, DAUGHTER OF ZION; BEHOLD, YOUR KING IS COMING, SEATED ON A DONKEY'S COLT."**

I am sure the praise here was louder than any standing ovation heard to date. Perhaps there has never been such heartfelt, Spirit-led worship. In the natural, they did not know He was coming as the Passover Lamb, but the Spirit surely knew. This is Spirit-led worship.

We praise Him by thanking Him for all that he has done for us.

Psalm 50:23

²³ **"He who offers a sacrifice of thanksgiving honors Me;**
And to him who orders *his* **way** *aright*
I shall show the salvation of God."

This passage also tells us that He will show those who order their way aright the salvation of God. Jesus is the salvation of God. *If* we want to see Him, *then* we need to make sure our lives line up with His teachings and that we are on the right pathway. Therefore, we can say that we praise the Lord with our actions and obedience.

Throughout this book, we will look at many of the Ten Commandments, especially those that tend to be overlooked or broken without remorse. Following are some commandments that we are wise to observe:

Exodus 20:7

⁷ "You shall not take the name of the LORD your God in vain, for the LORD will not leave him unpunished who takes His name in vain.

This is the third commandment. We need to keep our lips clean. When we have a slip of the tongue, we need to be quick to confess and ask the Lord for forgiveness. We should be quick to repent, since He is quick to forgive. Before we know it, we will have clean mouths.

Exodus 20:8-10

⁸ "Remember the sabbath day, to keep it holy. ⁹ Six days you shall labor and do all your work, ¹⁰ but the seventh day is a sabbath of the LORD your God; *in it* you shall not do any work, you or your son or your daughter, your male or your female servant or your cattle or your sojourner who stays with you.

This is the fourth of the Ten Commandments. It is not a suggestion. God rested on the seventh day of creation. Jesus observed the Sabbath rest. We need a day of rest to keep physically, spiritually and emotionally healthy. Observe the Sabbath rest and praise the Lord for it and through it. This is the only commandment with instructions. It is also a form of worship.

If we want to be all that He designed us to be, then we need to obey all of His commandments. This is made possible and even desirable through the indwelling Holy Spirit.

Let's look at another form of worship through our actions and obedience.

Luke 3:21-22

21 Now when all the people were baptized, Jesus was also baptized, and while He was praying, heaven was opened, 22 and the Holy Spirit descended upon Him in bodily form like a dove, and a voice came out of heaven, "You are My beloved Son, in You I am well-pleased."

Water baptism is our way of publicly confessing our walk with the Lord. Follow in the Lord's footsteps and be baptized. Surely the Father will be as well-pleased with you as He was with His Son.

The Lord is worthy of all our praise. He responds to it and it ushers in His Presence quicker than anything. The Lord inhabits the praises of His people. A few of the benefits are favor, peace, comfort and joy. Praise Him when you are joyful or grieved, rich or poor, healthy or sick, He will comfort you and supply your need.

The Lord also exults and rejoices over us! It is a two-way street.

Zephaniah 3:17

17 "The LORD your God is in your midst,
A victorious warrior.
He will exult over you with joy,
He will be quiet in His love,
He will rejoice over you with shouts of joy.

Begin to praise Him on a daily basis through song and obedience.

Let's praise Him, for He is our firm Foundation on Whom we build our lives. We are His dwelling place. We are the temple of the Holy Spirit. Praise the Lord, for He is worthy!

Fairest Lord Jesus

Fairest Lord Jesus, Ruler of all nature,
O Thou of God and man the Son,
Thee will I cherish, Thee will I honor,
Thou, my soul's glory, joy and crown.

Fair are the meadows, fairer still the woodlands,
Robed in the blooming garb of spring;
Jesus is fairer, Jesus is purer,
Who makes the woeful heart to sing.

Fair is the sunshine,
Fairer still the moonlight,
And all the twinkling starry host;
Jesus shines brighter, Jesus shines purer
Than all the angels heaven can boast.

All fairest beauty, heavenly and earthly,
Wondrously, Jesus, is found in Thee;
None can be nearer, fairer or dearer,
Than Thou, my Savior, art to me.

Beautiful Savior! Lord of all the nations!
Son of God and Son of Man!
Glory and honor, praise, adoration,
Now and forever more be Thine.

Anonymous

DAY 8

OPPOSITION

Opposition; the relation between two positions having the same subject and predicate but differing in quantity and/or quality; hostile or contrary action or condition; something that opposes; specifically: a body of persons opposing something; often capitalized: a political party opposing and prepared to replace the party in power.

The Israelites are praising the Lord because the foundation of the Temple has been laid. Everything seems to be going as planned. At the same time, however, their enemies heard about their progress and were not happy about it. Today, we'll see that their enemies had a plan of their own.

Opposition almost always follows a victory. Once we've set the foundation to build our lives on, we most likely will encounter opposition. Let's see what it looks like and how we should deal with it.

Ezra 4:1-3

¹ Now when the enemies of Judah and Benjamin heard that the people of the exile were building a temple to the LORD God of Israel, ² they approached Zerubbabel and the heads of fathers' *households*, and said to them, "Let us build with you, for we, like

you, seek your God; and we have been sacrificing to Him since the days of Esarhaddon king of Assyria, who brought us up here." **³ But Zerubbabel and Jeshua and the rest of the heads of fathers' *households* of Israel said to them, "You have nothing in common with us in building a house to our God; but we ourselves will together build to the LORD God of Israel, as King Cyrus, the king of Persia has commanded us."**

Zerubbabel and the heads of the fathers' households knew the Word of God and the history of Israel. These men were groomed to be the spiritual leaders of their families. They were respected men of God who had spiritual discernment. They were determined to restore the temple and at the same time, to keep their families safe and in right standing with God. The Temple was to be God's holy dwelling place. There were strict rules concerning who could go inside it. Therefore, the hands that were to build it were to be holy as well. This is why they were careful regarding those whom they allowed to help with its restoration.

Zerubbabel and the heads of households responded, "You have nothing in common with us." Our enemies today don't have anything in common with us, either. For us to experience the fullness of God's promise in our lives, we need to make sure that those who are with us are truly for us. God's enemies will try to thwart God's plans. We are responsible for knowing who they are and for keeping them out in order to protect that which God has entrusted to us. We need discernment.

Today, the Lord is looking for us to take our responsibility as the heads of our households seriously, regardless of our previous spiritual grooming. We are at a place where most of us have become so complacent and tolerant, that we no longer want to address the fact that our enemies even exist. Perhaps they are more wicked and determined than ever before.

Because Israel knew the Word of God and their history, they knew their enemies. How many times have we allowed others to thwart God's plan for our lives? This becomes evident when blessings seem to skip over us. Nothing seems to go as planned. Everything takes longer than anticipated, and the end results fall short of the original plan. When life becomes a constant struggle or striving becomes the norm, then it's time to step back and take a look at those involved. You will see when the troubles began and who entered into the picture at that same time. They could be very nice people, but for some reason the Lord doesn't want you with them. The Lord wants us to put our trust in Him and in Him alone. *If* we are putting our trust in others or have aligned ourselves with the wrong people, *then* surely He will allow our plans to fall short of His best. Separate yourself from these people and watch things come into place for you, as they should have all along.

For me, it was as if everyone in my life had been working together to keep me away from God. Even though it wasn't deliberate, because I was walking on the wrong path, it was true. I had to separate myself from all of my friends. I knew I had to become strong in my walk with the Lord before I would be strong enough to resist the temptations that I would encounter, when I witnessed His faithfulness to them. I disconnected my phone. At times, I parked my car around the block and then walked home to make my house look like I wasn't there, in order to separate myself from them.

It was hard to do, because they were my friends and we had helped each other out for years. Most of them are nice people. During this time, some of them encouraged me in my walk with the Lord. Others stood by at a distance, watching and waiting for me to fall to temptation and away from the Lord. I am grateful to say this didn't happen. Instead, it made me that much more determined to show them how faithful my God is. I still hope that each and every one of them makes a personal decision to give their lives to Christ. Many of them have already done that.

Since then, I have learned that even our Christian friends can keep us from fulfilling the plans the Lord has for us. We are not all called into the same ministries, church or denomination. We have to continuously make sure we are where we are supposed to be. We can't allow our friendships to hold us back. We are not always able to bring them with us, either.

Israel's enemies were bold and came with sweet words, "Let us build with you, for we, like you, seek your God.. When people offer to help us, we are more apt to accept it than not, never giving any thought to who they are or why they want to get involved in our work. This needs to change. We need to practice discernment so we can learn who our enemies are, or we'll never fully receive the promises of God. Those who oppose us will most likely appear to be nice people. Satan himself is the smoothest talker around. He is extremely charismatic and very attractive. This is a warning to us. When people appear to be too good to be true, they usually are. Learn to walk in wisdom. Know whom you are letting into your inner circle and pray for wisdom regarding your involvement with them.

We serve a jealous God and we are to have no other gods before Him. If someone is not for the Lord, they are against Him. Inevitably, their anger toward Him will come out and be seen in the turmoil they cause. Surround yourself with people who have the same goals and beliefs as you. Then you will be in a place of blessing.

Israel refused to allow their enemies to help them with the restoration of the Temple. Let's see how they responded to Israel's decision.

Ezra 4:4-6

⁴ Then the people of the land discouraged the people of Judah, and frightened them from building, ⁵ and hired counselors against them to frustrate their counsel all the days of Cyrus king of Persia, even until the reign of Darius king of Persia.

⁶ Now in the reign of Ahasuerus, in the beginning of his reign, they wrote an accusation against the inhabitants of Judah and Jerusalem.

We see here that their enemies didn't give up. They not only discouraged and frightened the Jews; they also hired counselors against them to frustrate their plans. They did this throughout the reign of both King Cyrus and King Artaxerxes, even until the reign of King Darius. The opposition that came against them was not a brief encounter; it went on for years. They seized every opportunity they had to come against Israel. They saw the reign of a new king as the perfect opportunity to get the work stopped. They determined to bring this new king onto their side by writing an accusation against Israel. The heads of households were right in their decision not to allow these men to participate in their work. Here we see that all along, their plan was to make sure the restoration of the Temple didn't happen. They knew that once the Temple was completed, the rest of Israel would soon return. They did not want that to happen.

In the following passage, we see that their enemies were already growing in number. (Those who are against us will always try to get as many people as they can to join them.)

Ezra 4:8-16

⁸ Rehum the commander and Shimshai the scribe wrote a letter against Jerusalem to King Artaxerxes, as follows— ⁹ then *wrote* Rehum the commander and Shimshai the scribe and the rest of their colleagues, the judges and the lesser governors, the officials, the secretaries, the men of Erech, the Babylonians, the men of

Susa, that is, the Elamites, [10] and the rest of the nations which the great and honorable Osnappar deported and settled in the city of Samaria, and in the rest of the region beyond the River. Now [11] this is the copy of the letter which they sent to him:

[11b] "To King Artaxerxes: Your servants, the men in the region beyond the River, and now [12] let it be known to the king that the Jews who came up from you have come to us at Jerusalem; they are rebuilding the rebellious and evil city and are finishing the walls and repairing the foundations. [13] Now let it be known to the king, that if that city is rebuilt and the walls are finished, they will not pay tribute, custom or toll, and it will damage the revenue of the kings. [14] Now because we are in the service of the palace, and it is not fitting for us to see the king's dishonor, therefore we have sent and informed the king, [15] so that a search may be made in the record books of your fathers. And you will discover in the record books and learn that that city is a rebellious city and damaging to kings and provinces, and that they have incited revolt within it in past days; therefore that city was laid waste. [16] We inform the king that if that city is rebuilt and the walls finished, as a result you will have no possession in *the province* beyond the River."

Remember, Israel had been rebellious. That was why God allowed King Nebuchadnezzar to take them captive to begin with. Their past has come back to haunt them. Let's see how Artaxerxes responded to the letter.

Ezra 4:17-22

[17] *Then* the king sent an answer to Rehum the commander, to Shimshai the scribe, and to the rest of their colleagues who live in Samaria and in the rest of *the provinces* beyond the River: "Peace. And now [18] the document which you sent to us has been translated and read before me. [19] A decree has been issued by me, and a search

has been made and it has been discovered that that city has risen up against the kings in past days, that rebellion and revolt have been perpetrated in it, [20] that mighty kings have ruled over Jerusalem, governing all *the provinces* beyond the River, and that tribute, custom and toll were paid to them. [21] So, now issue a decree to make these men stop *work*, that this city may not be rebuilt until a decree is issued by me. [22] Beware of being negligent in carrying out this *matter*; why should damage increase to the detriment of the kings?"

Not only has the past come back to haunt them, but it is also going to hinder them from moving forward.

Ezra 4: 23-24

[23] Then as soon as the copy of King Artaxerxes' document was read before Rehum and Shimshai the scribe and their colleagues, they went in haste to Jerusalem to the Jews and stopped them by force of arms.

[24] Then work on the house of God in Jerusalem ceased, and it was stopped until the second year of the reign of Darius king of Persia.

Their enemies didn't waste any time in stopping the work. They went in haste and stopped the Jews by force. But there is good news; another king is coming.

There will surely be opposition throughout our lives. We can expect to have our past failures to come back and haunt us. However, this is not an excuse not to stop moving forward. We cannot allow our fears to keep us from the work the Lord has called us to do. We need to trust that He has made provision for us. There will always be those who oppose us and, especially, our stand for Christ. There will also be those who stand so firm on the law that they are blinded to God's mercy and grace. However, there will also be those who stand firm on mercy and grace, who blatantly disrespect the law. We will be wise to seek the Lord's counsel through His Word, prayer and fasting before we plant our feet too firmly. We can be manipulated through religious beliefs as easily as through the world. There are as many people deceived by the many religions of the world as by the lusts of it.

Unless we know the voice of the Lord and follow Him alone, we can become religious tyrants or fall to the schemes of the world. Either way, we will not be successful in our walk with the Lord. Jesus said, "My sheep know My voice." If it isn't Jesus you are following, you are being led astray. He is the Good Shepherd. We are His sheep. Today, there are many who claim to be the Lord's, but have never heard His voice. This is a problem. We need to learn His voice. This is done by spending time with Him in His Word and through prayer. He desires more than anything to lead us through our life's journey. When we are led by Him, there is no end to His goodness. We will have peace, contentment and joy, even when no one around us does. This is because we put our trust and confidence in Him, not in ourselves or the things of the world.

The Bible says, "Many are called but few are chosen." We are responsible for preparing ourselves for His call. When we open our Bible, we need to pray for the Holy Spirit to bring it to life. He will illumine it so that we see it in a way that applies to us for that day. The Bible is the Living Word. Never read it without praying for the guidance and teaching of the Holy Spirit. Reading the Bible is how we learn the voice of the Lord and become intimate with Him. He will become more real to us than any problem or person in our lives. We will gain confidence to stand up to those who oppose us. We will learn how to become empty vessels the Lord speaks through. The Bible says, "When you are brought before the king, you will not worry about what to say, because the Lord will speak through you." Time with the Lord is where our peace and confidence come from.

Today, our hearts are God's dwelling place. Instead of us going into the Holy of Holies, the Holy One comes into our hearts and abides there forever. So we need to be careful about whom we allow into our lives, so that the world doesn't come in and pollute our Bible-based beliefs. Today, there are people who are rewriting the Bible, taking out the parts they don't like, the parts that reveal their sin. This is why the Lord so carefully instructed the Israelites to protect themselves and their families from outside influences. Today, the world is determined to tear down our belief system. We are to be different and to live our lives according to what God wants. He wants us to be at peace and made whole, no longer broken and torn down by deception and hurtful people. We must be careful of what we allow others to convince us of. We must know the truth, and it is found in the Word of God, the Holy Bible.

Opposition will come, but the Lord's desire is to turn their hearts toward Him. "He wishes that none should perish but all would have eternal life."

Zechariah 9:6b-7

6b And I will cut off the pride of the Philistines.

7 And I will remove their blood from their mouth
And their detestable things from between their teeth.
Then they also will be a remnant for our God,
And be like a clan in Judah,
And Ekron like a Jebusite.

This passage states that the Philistines will be like a clan in Judah. It was never God's plan or desire for anyone to hate Christians or Jews. His plan was, and is, for all of us to become His children, chosen by Him for His purposes. Jesus made this possible.

1 John 2:2

² and He Himself is the propitiation for our sins; and not for ours only, but also for *those of* the whole world.

I look forward to the day when the blinders are removed and truth is revealed to all those who've been deceived by religious tyrants. For very soon, we are going to see the King. Prepare yourselves.

The best offense for opposition is to live a holy life. Then there is nothing that can be held against us. Avoid secrets and live your life as an open book for all to see. Then you will be above reproach.

Our response to opposition should be as King David's was in the following verses: to praise the Lord and give Him the glory He deserves.

Psalm 63:7-8

⁷ For You have been my help,
And in the shadow of Your wings I sing for joy.

⁸ My soul clings to You;
Your right hand upholds me.

Jesus is our help and protection. Get under His wing and sing for joy. Cling to Him, and His right hand will hold you up in the day of opposition.

O How I Love Jesus

There is a Name I love to hear,
I love to sing its worth;
It sounds like music in my ear,
The sweetest Name on earth.
Refrain

O how I love Jesus,
O how I love Jesus,
O how I love Jesus,
Because He first loved me!

It tells me of a Savior's love,
Who died to set me free;
It tells me of His precious blood,
The sinner's perfect plea.

Refrain

It tells me of a Father's smile
Beaming upon His child;
It cheers me through this little while,
Through desert, waste, and wild.

Refrain

It tells me what my Father hath
In store for every day,
And though I tread a darksome path,
Yields sunshine all the way.

Refrain

It tells of One whose loving heart
Can feel my deepest woe;

ENCOURAGEMENT

Encouragement: the act of encouraging, something that encourages;
Encourage: to inspire with courage, spirit of hope; to spur on;
to give help or patronage to; suggests the raising of
one's confidence, especially by an external agency.

Encouraging words give hope and promise. The Bible gives us courage to carry on in the ways of the Lord. It reminds us that He is with us and will never leave nor forsake us. The Holy Spirit is our number-one Encourager.

Let's get back to our story and see how the Jews are doing under all the opposition. We left them very disappointed, as they were forced to stop the restoration of the Temple under King Artaxerxes' rule. We'll start by reading the verse we ended.

Ezra 4:24

²⁴ Then work on the house of God in Jerusalem ceased, and it was stopped until the second year of the reign of Darius king of Persia.

Artaxerxes is no longer king. Darius is now the King of Persia.

Ezra 5:1-2

¹ When the prophets, Haggai the prophet and Zechariah the son of

Iddo, prophesied to the Jews who were in Judah and Jerusalem in the name of the God of Israel, who was over them, ² then Zerubbabel the son of Shealtiel and Jeshua the son of Jozadak arose and began to rebuild the house of God which is in Jerusalem; and the prophets of God were with them supporting them.

Ezra tells us that Haggai and Zechariah prophesied to the Jews during this time of discouragement. When they prophesied, it was as though God Himself were speaking directly to Israel. Ezra doesn't divulge what was said by the prophets. We know they were encouraged, however, because afterwards, they arose and began to rebuild the house of God and the prophets stayed and supported them.

Let's take another look into the books of Haggai and Zechariah, to see just what was spoken.

Haggai 2:4-9

⁴ But now take courage, Zerubbabel,' declares the LORD, 'take courage also, Joshua son of Jehozadak, the high priest, and all you people of the land take courage,' declares the LORD, 'and work; for I am with you,' declares the LORD of hosts. ⁵ 'As for the promise which I made you when you came out of Egypt, My Spirit is abiding in your midst; do not fear!' ⁶ For thus says the LORD of hosts, 'Once more in a little while, I am going to shake the heavens and the earth, the sea also and the dry land. ⁷ I will shake all the nations; and they will come with the wealth of all nations, and I will fill this house with glory,' says the LORD of hosts. ⁸ 'The silver is Mine and the gold is Mine,' declares the LORD of hosts. ⁹ 'The latter glory of this house will be greater than the former,' says the LORD of hosts, 'and in this place I will give peace,' declares the LORD of hosts."

Through Haggai, the Lord speaks to the Jews and tells them,

"Take courage and work for I am with you." This is a green light, so to speak. These Words gave them the courage they needed to start working. He then said, "My Spirit is abiding in your midst; do not fear!" He is with them. Therefore, they are to be fearless. The Lord tells them of the future blessings and provision He has for them. He reminds them that the silver and gold in the world are His. He promises to shake the world, so the nations in it will bring them their wealth. He will fill the house with glory. The latter glory of this house will be greater than the former, and in it He will give peace. They now are fearless and filled with hope for the future.

Now, let's look at the words that Zechariah spoke.

Zechariah 4:6-9

⁶ Then he said to me, "This is the word of the LORD to Zerubbabel saying, 'Not by might nor by power, but by My Spirit,' says the LORD of hosts. ⁷ 'What are you, O great mountain? Before Zerubbabel *you will* become a plain; and he will bring forth the top stone with shouts of "Grace, grace to it!"'"

⁸ Also the word of the LORD came to me, saying, ⁹ "The hands of Zerubbabel have laid the foundation of this house, and his hands will finish *it*. Then you will know that the LORD of hosts has sent me to you.

Here, the Lord is saying to Zerubbabel through Zechariah that his victory will come by His Spirit; not by might or by power. He speaks to the mountain as though it is nothing, saying it will become a plain.

Mountains represent the obstacles in our lives, many of which appear so big that we begin to believe we'll never get past them. The Lord is saying to Zerubbabel, My Spirit will remove the obstacles in your life. They will no longer be seen. God also encourages him by letting him know he will bring forth the capstone (the top stone) with shouts of "Grace, grace to it!" In other words, Zerubbabel will see the building of the Temple through to completion. His hands laid the foundation and his hands will set the capstone.

Zechariah says "Then you will know that the LORD of hosts has sent me to you." This tells me that Zechariah was proving himself to be a true prophet of God.

Now that we know what the prophets had to say, it's time to get back to our story.

Ezra 5:3-5

³ At that time Tattenai, the governor of *the province* beyond the River, and Shethar-bozenai and their colleagues came to them and spoke to them thus, "Who issued you a decree to rebuild this temple and to finish this structure?" ⁴ Then we told them accordingly what the names of the men were who were reconstructing this building. ⁵ But the eye of their God was on the elders of the Jews, and they did not stop them until a report could come to Darius, and then a written reply be returned concerning it.

While the Jews are rebuilding the Temple, the governor comes by with his colleagues to see who issue'd the decree permitting them to rebuild. The builders boldly answer. However, the outcome is different this time. The eye of their God is on them, and they receive favor. Tattenai and his colleagues did not stop them. So they were allowed to work until King Darius received their report and replied to it.

The Words of Haggai and Zechariah are as encouraging as one could ask for. Let them resonate into your very being. Once we are born again, the Spirit abides in us and promises never to leave us. We must continue in the work of building the body of Christ until He returns to take us all home to glory. We have nothing to fear because "Greater is He who is in us, than he who is in the world (I John 4:4)."

This verse refers to the Holy Spirit in us, versus Satan who is in the world. We need to persevere and finish the race we began, for He is with us. In these passages, He calls Himself the Lord of hosts; this, too, should embolden the fearful. The Lord of hosts is the Lord of angels. These are warring angels who fight for us.

When we are being pressed down, there is nothing more encouraging than reminders of who our God is and that He is with us. He is the Creator of heaven and earth. He is All Knowing. He owns everything; the world is His. He is Faithful and True. He is our Provider and Protector. He is the Alpha and the Omega, the beginning and the end. Therefore, He goes before us and behind us. He is our Number-One Encourager. He is the Lord of Hosts. He is our Friend and our soon-coming King.

We must never forget that He is with us and that He holds the future in His hands. He will never lead us down a path of destruction. We can put our trust in Him, because He is Trustworthy. When He speaks to us through His Word or a person, we can rest assured what He has said will come to pass as long as we remain obedient to His call. We will slip and fall, but He is there to pick us up, dust us off and point us back in the right direction.

It is very important to learn how to discern the voice of the Lord, for there are false prophets. We must line every word up with the Bible and get confirmation by two or more people, one being ourself. *If* the word is from the Lord, *then* peace will follow. The Holy Spirit will also remind you of other times the same word was spoken to you. God's real Word will never return void, regardless of who speaks it. A true prophetic Word will stick to you like glue. You'll never forget it. It will reside in your very being.

When you need encouragement, look back on your life and ask the Holy Spirit to remind you of any prophetic Words that have been spoken over you. You will be reminded of things people have told you throughout your life. If you still remember them and they are encouraging, then take hold of them and ask the Lord to fulfill them. If you remember curses, rebuke them in the name of Jesus and ask Him to level them as a mountain to a plain. Ask Him to encourage you and restore to you the things the locust has eaten (Joel). This speaks of the things that have been taken from you throughout your life. Then get back to the work you once began so that you, too, may see it completed.

The Lord still speaks through prophets. We must not be ignorant regarding spiritual gifts. We all have them and need to understand how to use them for His glory. Let's take a quick look at what Paul had to say about this.

I Corinthians 14:1

¹ Pursue love, yet desire earnestly spiritual *gifts*, but especially that you may prophesy.

We are to earnestly desire the gift of prophecy even more than the other gifts. Spiritual gifts are given to help us. They are a gift from God. I personally want everything He has available for me to help me on this journey. Be encouraged; the Lord is still talking to His people.

Standing on the Promises

Standing on the promises of Christ my King,
Through eternal ages let His praises ring,
Glory in the highest, I will shout and sing,
Standing on the promises of God.

Refrain

Standing, standing,
Standing on the promises of God my Savior;
Standing, standing,
I'm standing on the promises of God.

Standing on the promises that cannot fail,
When the howling storms of doubt and fear assail,
By the living Word of God I shall prevail,
Standing on the promises of God.

Refrain

Standing on the promises I now can see
Perfect, present cleansing in the blood for me;
Standing in the liberty where Christ makes free,
Standing on the promises of God.

Refrain

Standing on the promises of Christ the Lord,
Bound to Him eternally by love's strong cord,
Overcoming daily with the Spirit's sword,
Standing on the promises of God.

Refrain

Standing on the promises I cannot fall,
Listening every moment to the Spirit's call
Resting in my Savior as my all in all,
Standing on the promises of God.

Refrain

Written by: R. Kelso Carter

DAY 10

PROVISION

Provision: The act or process of providing;
the fact or state of being prepared beforehand;
a measure taken beforehand to deal with a need or contingency;
a stock of needed materials or supplies.
Provide, providere (Latin): literally to see ahead;
To take precautionary measures;
"provide for the common defense." United States Constitution.

In this chapter, we are going to see how God went before Israel and provided for their every need. Preparations were made beforehand to insure the completion of the Temple. We will also look at the precautionary measures that were taken which provided the defense necessary to restrain their enemies once and for all.

We saw that their enemies were real and had grown in number. However, Israel's God was real, too. He sent them Words of encouragement through the prophets, which strengthened and emboldened them to arise and rebuild the Temple. Then, they received favor from Gov. Tattenai and his colleagues to continue the work until Darius could reply to their report.

Let's look at the beginning of this report.

Ezra 5:7-8

⁷ They sent a report to him in which it was written thus: "To Darius the king, all peace. ⁸ Let it be known to the king that we have gone to the province of Judah, to the house of the great God, which is being built with huge stones, and beams are being laid in the walls; and this work is going on with great care and is succeeding in their hands."

Those who wrote the first letter, written to Artaxerxes, lived in Judah and saw the Israelites as a threat to them and their land. However, here we see that Tattenai and his colleagues went to Judah, they do not live there. They call the Temple "the house of the great God." They report that the work on it is being done with great care. It sounds like they have an ally. The rest of the report is based on the words of the elders of Israel, and are a bold, humble and honest account of the temple and the Jewish people (Ezra 5:11-17). Let's read how Darius responds to them.

Ezra 6:1- 5

¹ Then King Darius issued a decree, and search was made in the archives, where the treasures were stored in Babylon. ² In Ecbatana in the fortress, which is in the province of Media, a scroll was found and there was written in it as follows: "Memorandum— ³ In the first year of King Cyrus, Cyrus the king issued a decree: '*Concerning* the house of God at Jerusalem, let the temple, the place where sacrifices are offered, be rebuilt and let its foundations be retained, its height being 60 cubits and its width 60 cubits; ⁴ with three layers of huge stones and one layer of timbers. And let the cost be paid from the royal treasury. ⁵ Also let the gold and silver utensils of the house of God, which Nebuchadnezzar took from the temple in Jerusalem and brought to Babylon, be returned and brought to their places in the temple in Jerusalem; and you shall put *them* in the house of God.'

King Darius acted wisely by looking back at the original decree in order to solve the dispute. He knew of the opposition Israel was contending with, and now saw clearly who was wrong and out of order. Let's see what he did with this new information.

Ezra 6:6-7

⁶ "Now *therefore*, Tattenai, governor of *the province* beyond the River, Shethar-bozenai and your colleagues, the officials of *the provinces* beyond the River, keep away from there. ⁷ Leave this work on the house of God alone; let the governor of the Jews and the elders of the Jews rebuild this house of God on its site.

Here, through King Darius the king of Persia, the Lord makes provision so the building of His temple can be completed. King Darius ordered Tattenai and all of his colleagues to keep away from the house of God. They were to allow them to rebuild the Temple on its original site.

King Darius also decided to make his own decree. Let's read it.

Ezra 6:8

⁸ Moreover, I issue a decree concerning what you are to do for these elders of Judah in the rebuilding of this house of God: the full cost is to be paid to these people from the royal treasury out of the taxes of *the provinces* beyond the River, and that without delay.

The taxes paid by those who opposed the Jews will now be used to provide for their every need. Originally, the royal treasury was going to pay for everything. Now it is specified that the royal treasury would pay, but from the taxes paid by the people in the provinces beyond the River. I'm sure at this point the people of these provinces were not happy with those who opposed the Jews. Things certainly didn't turn out the way their enemies had planned.

And there were even more provisions made. God made

provisions for the future maintenance of the temple. Their needs would be met daily.

Ezra 6:9, 10

⁹ Whatever is needed, both young bulls, rams, and lambs for a burnt offering to the God of heaven, and wheat, salt, wine and anointing oil, as the priests in Jerusalem request, *it* **is to be given to them daily without fail, ¹⁰ that they may offer acceptable sacrifices to the God of heaven and pray for the life of the king and his sons.**

In his reading, King Darius noticed the reason why King Cyrus wanted and allowed the temple to be rebuilt. He wanted the covering of the Lord through the prayers and sacrifices of the Jewish people. King Darius also knew of the many miracles this God had done throughout the ages. Now he had a chance to receive blessings from Him, for himself and his sons. He was determined, and I'm sure, grateful, that the dwelling place of the God of Israel was being built during his reign. He saw to it that nothing was going to stop this from happening. He issued yet another decree.

Ezra 6:11-12

¹¹ And I issued a decree that any man who violates this edict, a timber shall be drawn from his house and he shall be impaled on it and his house shall be made a refuse heap on account of this. ¹² May the God who has caused His name to dwell there overthrow any king or people who attempts to change it, so as to destroy this house of God in Jerusalem. I, Darius, have issued *this* **decree, let** *it* **be carried out with all diligence!"**

King Darius made sure that no one got in the way of the restoration of the Temple, by sentencing them to death if they did.

What can we learn from this? Before we commit ourselves to something, we need to know two things. First, did the plan come from the Lord? Second, does He want us involved in it? This is accomplished through prayer. If we jump in not knowing the Lord's will, we may find ourselves on a journey of tyranny, in a place of striving. The Bible says we are to wait upon the Lord. We shouldn't make any commitments without first going to the Lord in prayer, then waiting for confirmation. Do not lie or manipulate things in order to get your plan approved. This is not from the Lord. Good things can and will keep you from God's best. It is of utmost importance to know that God is leading you, if you want to receive the full blessing. He is always with us, but how we respond to His guidance is our decision. Are we following Him? Or are we dragging Him into our own plans then expecting Him to do what we want? He is way too big for that. Don't put the Lord your God to the test. Wait upon Him and see that He is good. Get into His perfect will and leave the striving for others.

Once we know we are being led by the Lord, we need to write a plan. Our plans need to be clear: who, what, when, where, why and how. These things need to be prayed through until peace resides inside us. This will assure us that we have the Lord's blessing and that He will see it to completion. Then, when opposition comes, we can look back at the original plans to see what the problem is and decide what we need to do to get back on track so we can complete the work we began.

Opposition will come. You will recognize it because it is divisive and controlling. Sometimes, it tries to take over and other times, it subtly moves in to hinder the work being done in the way the Lord wants it done. However it is working, the opposition must be removed as soon as possible. This is because it will quickly increase in numbers, bringing division and discord. People without a vision have a tendency to want to take over the work a visionary began. Stand your ground and don't let that happen. The Lord is looking for people who are willing to fight for what He has called them to do. Don't quit when opposition comes. The Lord has gone before you and will see you through it all. The battle is His and He is victorious. Fight the good fight.

We can rest assured that if we persevere, we will see the plans of our enemies revealed. We must never worry about where our provision is coming from. We only need to keep our eyes on our Provider and be obedient to the work He has given us. He owns the cattle on a thousand hills. He will provide for His own. This is a promise we can cling to. Be anxious for nothing! Wait upon the Lord. He will make a way where there seems to be no way. Our God is an awesome God, and He has gone before us.

The Lord has provided for me. He has led me every step of the way. He has given me clear instruction in the ministry. He showed me exactly how He wanted me to run things, where the funds were coming from and who was to help me. When I directed a homeless ministry, He let me know when to open the door, when to have showers and coffee and even what to cook. This ministry was successful because it was led by the Lord. We started with thirty-five men and three years later, we finished with one man left. I trust he has since given his life fully to the Lord and has been restored. The others had all been restored. We got the "Well done, good and faithful servant" comment. There was a lot of opposition. However, I had a written plan, and when opposition came, I was wise enough to go back to it and see where it was coming from. Once I made the change needed, we were back on track again. We did put up a great fight. I am glad He gave me the wisdom to do it His way, not mine or anyone else's.

We need to remember why the work was started. The purpose of the Temple was to offer prayer and sacrifices to God. Prayer and sacrifice usher in the presence of the Lord. In His presence is where we need to be. This is where He talks to us. He opens our eyes so we can see through His. He unstops our ears so we can hear as He does. This is where He reveals His heart for the lost and the hurting, those in bondage and despair. This is where He will give us an encouraging Word for ourselves or someone else. We are a work in progress. We are the Temple of God. He will see us through to completion. He is our Provider. He will make sure our needs are met daily. It is His will that we bring Him glory in all that we do. This can only be done when we are following His lead.

We have been deceived to think that God doesn't care about our lives and our plans. This is a lie from the pit of hell. Don't fall for it. Determine not to do anything without prayer. This is how accidents and mistakes are prevented. We are not alone. He is with us and wants to lead us into a place of peace and abundance. He is the same today as He was yesterday and will be tomorrow. He is Faithful and True. Take His hand and begin to walk in His perfect will.

Put your trust in Him for He is trustworthy. He is Jehovah–Jireh, the Lord who provides.

His Eye Is On the Sparrow

Why should I feel discouraged, why should the shadows come,
Why should my heart be lonely, and long for heaven and home,
When Jesus is my portion? My constant friend is He:
His eye is on the sparrow, and I know He watches me;
His eye is on the sparrow, and I know He watches me.

Refrain

I sing because I'm happy,
I sing because I'm free,
For His eye is on the sparrow,
And I know He watches me.

"Let not your heart be troubled," His tender word I hear,
And resting on His goodness, I lose my doubts and fears;
Though by the path He leadeth, but one step I may see;
His eye is on the sparrow, and I know He watches me;
His eye is on the sparrow, and I know He watches me.

Refrain

Whenever I am tempted, whenever clouds arise,
When songs give place to sighing, when hope within me dies,
I draw the closer to Him, from care He sets me free;
His eye is on the sparrow, and I know He watches me;
His eye is on the sparrow, and I know He watches me.

Refrain

Written by: Mrs. L.D. Martin

DAY 11

SACRIFICE

Sacrifice: An act of offering to a deity something precious;
the killing of a victim on an altar;
Something offered in sacrifice.
Destruction or surrender of something for the sake of something else;
something given up or lost.
Self-sacrifice: sacrifice of oneself or one's interest
for others or for a cause or ideal.

Today, we're going to compare Old Testament sacrifice to New Testament sacrifice.

Let's first look at the sacrifice King Darius made.

Ezra 6:13

¹³ Then Tattenai, the governor of the province beyond the River, Shethar-bozenai and their colleagues carried out the decree with all diligence, just as King Darius had sent.

We know King Darius did not leave room for misunderstanding. He clearly saw the hatred toward the Jews from those under his authority and demanded submission from them. He used his authority to properly uphold the law and to insure the safety of all his people. King Darius willingly sacrificed his popularity among those under him for the good of his kingdom.

Today, we see this type of hatred creeping into our own societies. We are constantly being told to be tolerant of other beliefs, when at the same time there's a gross intolerance to anything about God or Jesus. When God and all that represents Him are removed from a society, Satan gains full dominion. He is the author of confusion and lies. He hates people more than anything. He is the promoter of suicide and murder. Discrimination and gross hatred are gaining ground world-wide. Rulers are publicly speaking of annihilating races. We need leaders who are willing to sacrifice their own popularity and make a stand for the people and things of God, insuring safety for all people. This type of sacrifice comes with great reward. He promises to protect and prosper us. This is why the USA was such a blessed nation. She had honored God and His laws, which are the Ten Commandments.

Let's look at the sacrifices made by those who chose to leave Babylon in order to rebuild the Temple in Jerusalem.

Ezra 6:14

¹⁴ And the elders of the Jews were successful in building through the prophesying of Haggai the prophet and Zechariah the son of Iddo. And they finished building according to the command of the God of Israel and the decree of Cyrus, Darius, and Artaxerxes king of Persia.

The Jews went through a lot of difficulties but persevered to the end. This was a sacrifice. They not only gave their time to God, but also gave up their own interests for His. For years, they gave up peace to be continuously tormented by their enemies. However, it did pay off. I'm sure most of them had doubts they'd ever see it to completion; regardless of the fact that the Prophets said they would. The job they began is finally finished, O' the joy that filled their hearts!

We must never lose heart in the midst of the work God gives us, either. He has promised to complete the good work He began and will never give us more than we can handle. When times get tough, look back and remember His promises and encouraging words. Never forget your purpose, and keep those who encourage you close by, as the Israelites did with the prophets. Determine to finish well. Those who oppose us will be defeated when we stay in God's perfect will. We are victorious in Jesus! It is extremely rewarding to sacrifice our time and interests for His purposes. There is nothing like it.

Now, let's look at the sacrifices being made as they celebrate the dedication of the temple.

Ezra 6:15-18

¹⁵ This temple was completed on the third day of the month Adar; it was the sixth year of the reign of King Darius. ¹⁶ And the sons of Israel, the priests, the Levites and the rest of the exiles, celebrated the dedication of this house of God with joy.

¹⁷ They offered for the dedication of this temple of God 100 bulls, 200 rams, 400 lambs, and as a sin offering for all Israel 12 male goats, corresponding to the number of the tribes of Israel.

¹⁸ Then they appointed the priests to their divisions and the Levites in their orders for the service of God in Jerusalem, as it is written in the book of Moses.

The Temple is officially restored. They are celebrating and dedicating their works to God, for His purposes and glory. This is a huge celebration. It involved a lot of work, due to the large number of sacrifices given. The priests and Levites were working nonstop. This was their call in life. It was a sacrifice of labor. Once the dedication and celebration was completed, the Jews appointed the priests and Levites for the service of God, according to the book of Moses.

The Temple had been defiled by pagans during the captivity.

Now, it needs to be purified. This was accomplished through the blood of the sacrifices. The blood purified the Temple and covered the sin of the entire nation of Israel.

What an incredible time this was. Even today, we can look back at this time in history and be reminded of God's faithfulness to His people.

Today, we also celebrate the completion of a building or a job well done. However, we often take the glory for ourselves and completely forget to honor the One who actually made it all happen. We are wise when we dedicate our works to God for His purposes and glory. This is an acceptable sacrifice and it insures us of His continued blessings. We no longer bring costly animals to sacrifice as a part of our celebration. Instead, we bring our tithe to the house of God. This is an acceptable sacrifice. In doing so, we give Him honor by acknowledging that all we have accomplished is due to His provision.

Give God the glory and know that He will lift you up in His perfect timing. We are not to lift ourselves up, because in doing so, we set ourselves up for a fall. Pride always goes before a fall.

The Temple was originally built by King Solomon, who was King David's son. Let's see what he and all the people offered to God as a sacrifice when they originally dedicated it to Him.

2 Chronicles 7:4-5

⁴ Then the king and all the people offered sacrifice before the LORD.

⁵ King Solomon offered a sacrifice of 22,000 oxen and 120,000 sheep. Thus the king and all the people dedicated the house of God.

Imagine the sound of all the animals and the smell in the air from the blood. Animal sacrifice for sin was not permanent. In fact, it was just one sin away from being useless. Then, another sacrifice would have to be made to cover that sin. God did not like to see all of these animals sacrificed. He had a better plan in store. Remember, He is all about life and life to its fullest. Cross references:

We'll now look at the New Testament to see why animal sacrifices are no longer necessary. Let's hear what John the Baptist declared about Jesus and sin, when Jesus went to him to be baptized.

John 1:29

²⁹ The next day he saw Jesus coming to him and said, "Behold, the Lamb of God who takes away the sin of the world!

This was the first time Jesus was publicly recognized as the Messiah, the long-awaited Lamb of God who would take away the sin of the world.

We know sin is still in the world. But once confessed, it is covered by the blood of the Lamb and cast away from us as far as the east is from the west.

The following passage is part of Jesus' prayer in the garden of Gethsemane, right before His betrayal. He is in Jerusalem to celebrate Passover.

Luke 22:42

⁴² saying, "Father, if You are willing, remove this cup from Me; yet not My will, but Yours be done."

Jesus agonized over the fact that He was about to become the cup of redemption, the last cup of the Passover feast. Through His death, burial and resurrection, He became our Redeemer. The Bible says that as Jesus prayed, He literally sweat blood. He knew He was the Passover Lamb. He knew everything He was about to go through. Jesus offered Himself as a living sacrifice and shed his blood for us. His blood is the only blood that can take away our sin and make us holy and acceptable to God. We are sanctified through His perfect, sinless blood. On the cross, He said, "It is finished." He is the final sacrifice. There is no reason for animal sacrifices any more. His blood redeemed us all.

If you have never seen the movie, "The Passion of the Christ," by Mel Gibson, I suggest you do so in order to better understand all that Christ went through for you. The movie is not for children. Its content is quite vivid.

Instead of sacrificing animals, we now sacrifice our natural lives for a supernatural life. We lay our lives down for Him who laid His down for us. We die to self in order to live in the Spirit. We crucify our fleshly desires daily to obtain His. The temple was the place where daily sacrifices were made. We, as the temple of the Holy Spirit, need to make daily sacrifices as well. We need to remove ourselves from the equation; then it will be all of Him and none of us. It cannot be a mix if you are seeking the Lord's very best for yourself. Natural or supernatural, it's a choice decided by us.

We need to retain Christ as our foundation. When we sacrifice the natural, the supernatural is resurrected in us. That is the Holy Spirit and He looks just like Jesus, our Foundation. This is how we'll know we are aligned with Him. We will look just like Him in our daily walk.

The more the Lord transforms you into His image, the more you'll realize how unimportant the things you wanted to hang on to are. It takes time, but when you look back, you'll notice how quickly it all happened. Put your trust in Him, and let go and let God.

Not only do we need to lay down our lives down as individuals, but we also need to lay down the corporate church. The Word of God needs to be its very foundation. There are specific qualifications that must be met for those placed in authority. The Bible is very clear regarding these qualifications. The church needs to sacrifice her agenda and get back to His, because He cannot bless a disobedient church.

Make sure you are in a church that is run according to God's Word, so you don't find yourself being deceived in very subtle ways. Take responsibility for your families and make sure your spiritual leaders are speaking the truth, the Word of God. Bring your Bible with you and read it for yourself. Don't assume what is being read is true. Let this be another sacrifice you give unto God. Be blessed!

I Surrender All

All to Jesus, I surrender;
All to Him I freely give;
I will ever love and trust Him,
In His presence daily live.

Refrain

I surrender all, I surrender all,
All to Thee, my blessèd Savior,
I surrender all.

All to Jesus I surrender;
Humbly at His feet I bow,
Worldly pleasures all forsaken;
Take me, Jesus, take me now.
Refrain

All to Jesus, I surrender;
Make me, Savior, wholly Thine;
Let me feel the Holy Spirit,
Truly know that Thou art mine.
Refrain

All to Jesus, I surrender;
Lord, I give myself to Thee;
Fill me with Thy love and power;
Let Thy blessing fall on me.
Refrain

All to Jesus I surrender;
Now I feel the sacred flame.
O the joy of full salvation!
Glory, glory, to His Name!
Refrain

Written by: Judson W. VanDeVenter

DAY 12

COMMUNION

Communion: an act or instance of sharing;
Communion: a Christian sacrament in which consecrated bread and
wine are consumed as memorials of Christ's death.

We have gained knowledge about how to recognize our opposition and to receive and give encouragement. We've learned the Lord is our Provider and know what He considers to be an acceptable sacrifice. Today, we are going to look at Communion.

First, let's get back to our story and see what is happening now that the Temple has been completed and dedicated.

Ezra 6:19

¹⁹ The exiles observed the Passover on the fourteenth of the first month.

Imagine the joy and thankfulness that filled the hearts of the Jews during this time. Passover is in remembrance of their exodus out of Egypt, when the Lord delivered their forefathers out of captivity. Now, they are observing it after their own captivity and exodus from Babylon.

In order to understand Passover better, we'll look at the book of

Exodus. Here, the Lord had sent Moses to tell Pharaoh to "Let my people go." But Pharaoh was not about to let them go, because he depended upon their labor way too much for that. So God began to send the ten plagues onto Egypt, one at a time. He did this to prove to Pharaoh that He was alive and well and very serious about seeing to it that His people were let go. However, Pharaoh still refused to let His people go.

Exodus 11:1, 4-7

¹ Now the LORD said to Moses, "One more plague I will bring on Pharaoh and on Egypt; after that he will let you go from here. When he lets you go, he will surely drive you out from here completely.

⁴ Moses said, "Thus says the LORD, 'About midnight I am going out into the midst of Egypt, ⁵ and all the firstborn in the land of Egypt shall die, from the firstborn of the Pharaoh who sits on his throne, even to the firstborn of the slave girl who is behind the millstones; all the firstborn of the cattle as well. ⁶ Moreover, there shall be a great cry in all the land of Egypt, such as there has not been *before* and such as shall never be again. ⁷ But against any of the sons of Israel a dog will not *even* bark, whether against man or beast, that you may understand how the LORD makes a distinction between Egypt and Israel.'

We all hate stories that have death in them. Unfortunately, however, death is the only thing that worked here. The Lord gave Pharaoh nine opportunities to let His people go before this plague was sent. The Lord hates death more than any of us. Remember, He is all about life and life to its fullest. However, when the God of Israel says enough is enough, He means it. It is important for us all to know that God does make a distinction between the world and Israel. Israel is the apple of His eye. However, the rest of us are adopted into the family through Jesus.

Now, let's take a look at how the Lord made provision for His people.

Exodus 12:1-7, 13, 42

¹ Now the LORD said to Moses and Aaron in the land of Egypt, ² "This month shall be the beginning of months for you; it is to be the first month of the year to you. ³ Speak to all the congregation of Israel, saying, 'On the tenth of this month they are each one to take a lamb for themselves, according to their fathers' households, a lamb for each household. ⁴ Now if the household is too small for a lamb, then he and his neighbor nearest to his house are to take one according to the number of persons *in them*; according to what each man should eat, you are to divide the lamb. ⁵ Your lamb shall be an unblemished male a year old; you may take it from the sheep or from the goats. ⁶ You shall keep it until the fourteenth day of the same month, then the whole assembly of the congregation of Israel is to kill it at twilight. ⁷ Moreover, they shall take some of the blood and put it on the two doorposts and on the lintel of the houses in which they eat it.

¹³ 'The blood shall be a sign for you on the houses where you live; and when I see the blood I will pass over you, and no plague will befall you to destroy you when I strike the land of Egypt.

⁴² It is a night to be observed for the LORD for having brought them out from the land of Egypt; this night is for the LORD, to be observed by all the sons of Israel throughout their generations.

The life of the firstborn of Israel was spared because of the blood of the lamb they applied to their door posts and lintel (door header). The Lord's directions were very clear, He covered the: who, what, when, where and why very well. He left no room for mistakes. This was a very serious thing that was happening. Their lives depended upon their obedience. It would be a night they would never forget.

To make sure the generations to come would understand what God did for them, there was to be an annual feast mandated by God Himself (v. 42). To this day, the Jews still observe Passover on the fourteenth day of their first month.

You can imagine the joy and thankfulness that filled their hearts as they observed Passover after being delivered from their captivity to Babylon. They knew with all of their being that it was God who went before them and put it on King Cyrus' heart to let His people go.

Let's get back to our story.

Ezra 6:20-21

20 For the priests and the Levites had purified themselves together; all of them were pure. Then they slaughtered the Passover *lamb* for all the exiles, both for their brothers the priests and for themselves. 21 The sons of Israel who returned from exile and all those who had separated themselves from the impurity of the nations of the land to *join* them, to seek the LORD God of Israel, ate *the Passover.*

The priests and the Levites had to purify themselves before they could even slaughter the Passover lamb. Their duties were not taken lightly. This was a time to remember all that God had done for them and His faithfulness to them. During this time, the people separated themselves from the sin of the nations. In doing so, they purified themselves.

The Israelites observed another feast at this time, as well.

Ezra 6:22

22 And they observed the Feast of Unleavened Bread seven days with joy, for the LORD had caused them to rejoice, and had turned the heart of the king of Assyria toward them to encourage them in the work of the house of God, the God of Israel.

The feast of Unleavened Bread began in Egypt at the same time as Passover.

Exodus 12:18-20

¹⁸ In the first *month*, on the fourteenth day of the month at evening, you shall eat unleavened bread, until the twenty-first day of the month at evening. ¹⁹ Seven days there shall be no leaven found in your houses; for whoever eats what is leavened, that person shall be cut off from the congregation of Israel, whether *he is* an alien or a native of the land. ²⁰ You shall not eat anything leavened; in all your dwellings you shall eat unleavened bread.'"

This, too, is a time of separation. They were to be found without sin, which is represented by leaven or "yeast," as we call it today. They would remove all the yeast from their houses before the first day of the feast and, as they did so, they would examine their lives for sin. They would reflect upon righteous living and the goodness of the Lord.

In the following passage, Jesus foretells the fulfillment of Passover and the Feast of Unleavened Bread and the Father's plan of redemption, eternal life.

John 6:41-58

⁴¹ Therefore the Jews were grumbling about Him, because He said, "I am the bread that came down out of heaven." ⁴² They were saying, "Is not this Jesus, the son of Joseph, whose father and mother we know? How does He now say, 'I have come down out of heaven'?" ⁴³ Jesus answered and said to them, "Do not grumble among yourselves. ⁴⁴ No one can come to Me unless the Father who sent Me draws him; and I will raise him up on the last day. ⁴⁵ It is written in the prophets, 'AND THEY SHALL ALL BE TAUGHT OF GOD.' Everyone who has heard and learned from the Father, comes to Me. ⁴⁶ Not that anyone has seen the Father, except the

One who is from God; He has seen the Father. ⁴⁷ Truly, truly, I say to you, he who believes has eternal life. ⁴⁸ I am the bread of life. ⁴⁹ Your fathers ate the manna in the wilderness, and they died. ⁵⁰ This is the bread which comes down out of heaven, so that one may eat of it and not die. ⁵¹ I am the living bread that came down out of heaven; if anyone eats of this bread, he will live forever; and the bread also which I will give for the life of the world is My flesh."

⁵² Then the Jews began to argue with one another, saying, "How can this man give us *His* flesh to eat?" ⁵³ So Jesus said to them, "Truly, truly, I say to you, unless you eat the flesh of the Son of Man and drink His blood, you have no life in yourselves. ⁵⁴ He who eats My flesh and drinks My blood has eternal life, and I will raise him up on the last day. ⁵⁵ For My flesh is true food, and My blood is true drink. ⁵⁶ He who eats My flesh and drinks My blood abides in Me, and I in him. ⁵⁷ As the living Father sent Me, and I live because of the Father, so he who eats Me, he also will live because of Me. ⁵⁸ This is the bread which came down out of heaven; not as the fathers ate and died; he who eats this bread will live forever."

Jesus is proclaiming a New Blood Covenant to come, one made with His flesh and blood. It will be observed in the partaking of the bread and wine of Holy Communion (v. 56), and whoever eats and drinks of it has eternal life (v. 54).

Let's see what Jesus says to His disciples during the last Passover feast that He ate with them.

Luke 22:14-20

¹⁴ When the hour had come, He reclined *at the table*, and the apostles with Him. ¹⁵ And He said to them, "I have earnestly desired to eat this Passover with you before I suffer; ¹⁶ for I say to you, I shall never again eat it until it is fulfilled in the kingdom of God." ¹⁷ And when He had taken a cup *and* given thanks, He said, "Take this and

share it among yourselves; [18] for I say to you, I will not drink of the fruit of the vine from now on until the kingdom of God comes." [19] And when He had taken *some* bread *and* given thanks, He broke it and gave it to them, saying, "This is My body which is given for you; do this in remembrance of Me." [20] And in the same way *He* took the cup after they had eaten, saying, "This cup which is poured out for you is the new covenant in My blood.

This was the last Passover Feast Jesus ate. He was fully aware that He was about to fulfill His purpose in life, which was becoming the Passover Lamb. He did not come to judge the world but to save it. He accomplished this through His perfect, sinless life which produced the blood that would cover the sin of the world once and for all. He knew that through His shed blood, all who would choose Him as their personal Lord and Savior would escape death and be given eternal life. He willfully laid Himself on the cross of Calvary so we could live. He is the long-awaited Messiah of the Jewish people. He is the Lamb of God without blemish, the final sacrifice.

We serve a pure God who cannot look upon sin. This is why Jesus on the cross cried, "Father, why have Thou forsaken Me." When He was on the cross, He literally took upon Himself the sin of the world. God had to look away from Him. This was the most agonizing part of the crucifixion for Christ, because the Father had never turned His back on Him before. He laid His life down for the Father's plan of redemption.

Just as the priests purified themselves, we need to purify ourselves before we partake in Holy Communion. We do this by confessing our sin. When we confess with a pure heart, our sin is removed from us as far as the east is from the west (Psalm 103:12). During Communion, we need to lay our lives down for His use as well. Holy Communion is only for those who have given their lives to the Lord by accepting Him as their personal Lord and Savior. The

Bible warns us not to take Communion if we are not born again. Our freedom from the captivity of sin came at a very high price.

Israel observed the feast of Unleavened Bread for seven days. We need to observe the Unleavened Bread, not just once a year, but seven days a week and fifty-two weeks a year. Jesus is the Unleavened Bread, the Bread of Life, the only life without sin. We are not to go through this life on our own, but with Jesus at our side on a day-to-day basis. Let Him be seen in all that you do by separating yourself from the sin of the world. Learn from the Feast of Unleavened Bread and cleanse your house of all sin, once and for all.

Communion is taken in remembrance of Jesus. The bread represents His sinless life, which He freely gave for us. The wine represents His blood which He poured out on the cross for us. His blood covers and protects us from the angel of death, as did the blood of the lamb on the door posts and lintel on that first Passover night. Through His blood, we have the assurance of eternal life. He did it all for you. Partake in Communion with reverence and a grateful heart.

He said, "Do this in remembrance of Me." Every time He sees us partaking in Holy Communion, joy fills His heart, because He knows He has not been forgotten. So partake in Communion with reverence and a grateful heart.

When I Survey the Wondrous Cross

When I survey the wondrous cross
On which the Prince of glory died,
My richest gain I count but loss,
And pour contempt on all my pride.

Forbid it, Lord, that I should boast,
Save in the death of Christ my God!
All the vain things that charm me most,
I sacrifice them to His blood.

See from His head, His hands, His feet,
Sorrow and love flow mingled down!
Did e'er such love and sorrow meet,
Or thorns compose so rich a crown?

His dying crimson, like a robe,
Spreads o'er His body on the tree;
Then I am dead to all the globe,
And all the globe is dead to me.

Were the whole realm of nature mine,
That were a present far too small;
Love so amazing, so divine,
Demands my soul, my life, my all

Written by: Isaac Watts

DAY 13
PRIEST

Priest: one authorized to perform sacred rites of a religion, especially as a mediatory agent between humans and God.

Today we will get a better understanding our priestly calling.

Ezra now enters our story. Artaxerxes is now the king of Persia. He is the son of the King Artaxerxes, who stopped the restoration of the Temple.

Ezra 7:1-5

¹ Now after these things, in the reign of Artaxerxes king of Persia, *there went up* Ezra son of Seraiah, son of Azariah, son of Hilkiah, ² son of Shallum, son of Zadok, son of Ahitub, ³ son of Amariah, son of Azariah, son of Meraioth, ⁴ son of Zerahiah, son of Uzzi, son of Bukki, ⁵ son of Abishua, son of Phinehas, son of Eleazar, son of Aaron the chief priest.

Here we learn that Ezra's family line goes back to Aaron, the chief priest. This passage establishes Ezra's priestly lineage.

Ezra 7:6

⁶ This Ezra went up from Babylon, and he was a scribe skilled in the law of Moses, which the LORD God of Israel had given; and the

king granted him all he requested because the hand of the LORD his God was upon him.

Ezra was one of the captives who lived in Babylon. He was a scribe skilled in the Law of Moses. The law was given to Moses by God Himself, not just any god, but the Lord God of Israel. This fact was accentuated because people were worshipping many false gods. We also see that God's hand was upon Ezra. Therefore, doors opened for him. In this case, we see that the king granted him all he requested. He was allowed to leave Babylon and go up to Jerusalem.

Let's see who went to Jerusalem with Ezra.

Ezra 7:7

⁷ Some of the sons of Israel and some of the priests, the Levites, the singers, the gatekeepers and the temple servants went up to Jerusalem in the seventh year of King Artaxerxes.

Besides the Jews, there were priests and Levites. The Levites were the singers, gatekeepers and temple servants. They were a team working together to glorify the Lord.

Ezra 7:8, 9

⁸ He came to Jerusalem in the fifth month, which was in the seventh year of the king. ⁹ For on the first of the first month he began to go up from Babylon; and on the first of the fifth month he came to Jerusalem, because the good hand of his God *was* upon him.

They arrived in Jerusalem after traveling for four months. The journey took five months. This was an exciting trip, since most of them were on their way to Jerusalem for the first time. The priests and the Levites had spent their lives preparing for this. The priests were excited about being able to perform their priestly duties in the Temple in Jerusalem for the first time.

Verse 9 ended with the statement, "The good hand of his God was upon him." In verse 10, we see why.

Ezra 7:10

¹⁰ For Ezra had set his heart to study the law of the LORD and to practice it, and to teach *His* statutes and ordinances in Israel.

Ezra prepared himself to teach the ways of the Lord to those in Israel.

Today, it should be important for us to know the hand of the Lord is upon us. Then we can be sure we're where we are supposed to be and doing what we are supposed to do. We can all look back on our lives and see the times when this happened. We can also see the times when it didn't. These situations reveal to us the importance of prayer and reading the Word of God, because doing these things will confirm God's will to us.

We must learn to be team players by encouraging and lifting others up, allowing them to minister in their specific calling, not by holding or pulling others down in order to lift ourselves up. The Lord is to be the One who exalts us. There is unity when we understand and put this into practice. Unity is of utmost importance in ministry.

Now that we better understand the priestly order of Aaron, we will look at the priestly order of Melchizedek. Melchizedek was the first priest of God Most High.

Gen. 14:18-19

¹⁸ And Melchizedek king of Salem brought out bread and wine; now he was a priest of God Most High. ¹⁹ He blessed him and said, "Blessed be Abram of God Most High, Possessor of heaven and earth;

Melchizedek, king of Salem, which means king of peace, brought bread and wine to Abram and blessed him. Abram's name was changed by God to Abraham. He was Levi's great-grandfather.

Following is a prophetic Psalm written by King David.

Psalm 110:1-4

¹ The LORD says to my Lord:
"Sit at My right hand Until I make Your enemies a footstool for Your feet."

² The LORD will stretch forth Your strong scepter from Zion, *saying*, **"Rule in the midst of Your enemies."**

³ Your people will volunteer freely in the day of Your power;
In holy array, from the womb of the dawn,
Your youth are to You as the dew.

⁴ The LORD has sworn and will not change His mind,
"You are a priest forever
According to the order of Melchizedek."

God the Father is talking to Jesus about His dominion and priestly calling. He tells Jesus to sit at His right hand, saying He will reign from there until His enemies are made a footstool at His feet. Jesus' people, Christians, will volunteer freely in holy array. The indwelling Holy Spirit is our holy array. He then tells Jesus, He is a priest forever, according to the order of Melchizedek, a priest with no beginning or end.

Let's read what the Apostle Paul had to say about Jesus.

Hebrews 5:7-10

⁷ In the days of His flesh, He offered up both prayers and supplications with loud crying and tears to the One able to save Him from death, and He was heard because of His piety. ⁸ Although He was a Son, He learned obedience from the things which He

suffered. ⁹ And having been made perfect, He became to all those who obey Him the source of eternal salvation, ¹⁰ being designated by God as a high priest according to the order of Melchizedek.

Paul was referring to Jesus' prayer in Gethsemane, right before He was betrayed by Judas Iscariot. His Father did not save Him from death. He was crucified. However, He rose from the grave on the third day, so we could have eternal life. Jesus is designated by God as a high priest according to the order of Melchizedek.

Jesus, our high Priest, brought bread and wine to His twelve disciples at the last supper. The bread and wine represent the new covenant between God and man. Jesus is the bridge that brings man to God.

It was the priests' duty to offer up the animal sacrifices to God. The animals' blood atoned for the sin of Israel. Once a year, on the Day of Atonement, a high priest would go behind the veil that separated them from God, into the Holy of Holies. The Holy of Holies was God's dwelling place. Inside was the mercy seat which sat upon the Ark of the Covenant. On the Day of Atonement, a priest would sprinkle blood upon the mercy seat to atone for the sin of Israel.

Jesus as the High Priest, offered Himself on the cross as the Lamb of God. His blood atoned for the sin of all mankind, once and for all. When God looks at us, who have accepted Jesus as our Lord and Savior, He sees Jesus' blood, not our sin.

Let's read what happened while Jesus was on the cross.

Luke 23:44-46

⁴⁴ It was now about the sixth hour, and darkness fell over the whole land until the ninth hour, ⁴⁵ because the sun was obscured; and the veil of the temple was torn in two. ⁴⁶ And Jesus, crying out with

a loud voice, said, "Father, INTO YOUR HANDS I COMMIT MY SPIRIT." Having said this, He breathed His last.

When Jesus was on the cross, the veil was ripped from top to bottom. God reached down from heaven and ripped it. Because of this, we can now approach God for ourselves through the blood of the Lamb. Jesus is our High Priest. He made a way for us to come to the mercy seat of God, which is the throne of grace. Jesus sits at the Father's right hand, always interceding for us. He is the way, the truth, and the life. No one comes to the Father except through Him.

Once washed in His blood, we can boldly come to the Father in prayer and make our petitions known. We are favored by God because we chose to believe in Jesus, His Son. He is the King of Kings. There is nothing we can't do, with Him on our side. Jesus fulfilled the duties of the priestly order. He was the final blood sacrifice. We now come directly to the Father in prayer. He is "a priest forever, according to the order of Melchizedek."

Today, Christians are called to be priests. In order to fulfill our calling, we need to set our hearts on learning God's Word, so we can put it into practice and teach it wherever the Lord leads us.

I Peter 2:4-5, 9-10

⁴ And coming to Him as to a living stone which has been rejected by men, but is choice and precious in the sight of God, ⁵ you also, as living stones, are being built up as a spiritual house for a holy priesthood, to offer up spiritual sacrifices acceptable to God through Jesus Christ.

⁹ But you are A CHOSEN RACE, A royal PRIESTHOOD, A HOLY NATION, A PEOPLE FOR *God's* OWN POSSESSION, so that you may proclaim the excellencies of Him who has called you out of darkness into His marvelous light; ¹⁰ for you once were NOT A PEOPLE, but now you are THE PEOPLE OF GOD; you

had NOT RECEIVED MERCY, but now you have RECEIVED MERCY.

The New American Standard Bible, which I'm using, capitalizes letters like we see here to indicate Old Testament quotations. These words were spoken through Moses and Isaiah.

Everyone who has not rejected Jesus, this Living Stone, is now a chosen race, a royal priesthood, a holy nation, a people for God's own possession. We are to offer up spiritual sacrifices to God through Jesus. We are to proclaim the excellencies of our Lord, telling about how He called us out of darkness into His marvelous light.

Jesus is our High Priest. He is over us. Submit yourself to Him and He will lead and guide you. He has an awesome plan for your life. Get into an in-depth Bible study so you can learn the Word of God. Apply it to your life until you are saturated. Open your heart up to His Word, and it will transform you into the person God designed you to be.

Like Ezra, when you become saturated in His Word and led by the Holy Spirit, those around you will know that the hand of the Lord is upon you. Only by God is one drawn to Jesus. Let go and let the Holy Spirit speak through you. You are a priest.

Channels Only

How I praise Thee, precious Savior,
That Thy love laid hold of me;
Thou hast saved and cleansed and filled me
That I might Thy channel be.

Refrain

Channels only, blessèd Master,
But with all Thy wondrous power
Flowing through us, Thou canst use us
Every day and every hour.

Just a channel full of blessing,
To the thirsty hearts around;
To tell out Thy full salvation
All Thy loving message sound.

Refrain

Emptied that Thou shouldest fill me,
A clean vessel in Thy hand;
With no power but as Thou givest
Graciously with each command.

Refrain

Witnessing Thy power to save me,
Setting free from self and sin;
Thou who boughtest to possess me,
In Thy fullness, Lord, come in.

Refrain

Jesus, fill now with Thy Spirit
Hearts that full surrender know;
That the streams of living water
From our inner self may flow.

Refrain

Written by: Mary E. Maxwell

DAY 14

REVERENCE

Reverence: honor or respect felt or shown;
a gesture of respect: the state of being revered.
Revere: to show devoted deferential honors to;
regard as worthy of great honor.

This week, we have gained knowledge about what to expect as Christians, from God and the world. There will be times of opposition, but encouragement will come. The Lord will provide for our every need. We first need to lay down our own lives as a living sacrifice in order for His life to be exalted in us.

Today, we will see what reverence looks like by looking at King Artaxerxes' decree concerning Ezra and the Temple of God in Jerusalem. As you read, make a mental note of the gestures of honor and respect he gives to the God of Israel, His Word, His house and His servants. He is an incredible example for all of us to follow. Imagine if the world leaders of today followed this example.

Ezra 7:11-26

¹¹ Now this is the copy of the decree which King Artaxerxes gave to Ezra the priest, the scribe, learned in the words of the commandments of the LORD and His statutes to Israel: ¹²

"Artaxerxes, king of kings, to Ezra the priest, the scribe of the law of the God of heaven, perfect *peace*. And now [13] I have issued a decree that any of the people of Israel and their priests and the Levites in my kingdom who are willing to go to Jerusalem, may go with you. [14] Forasmuch as you are sent by the king and his seven counselors to inquire concerning Judah and Jerusalem according to the law of your God which is in your hand, [15] and to bring the silver and gold, which the king and his counselors have freely offered to the God of Israel, whose dwelling is in Jerusalem, [16] with all the silver and gold which you find in the whole province of Babylon, along with the freewill offering of the people and of the priests, who offered willingly for the house of their God which is in Jerusalem; [17] with this money, therefore, you shall diligently buy bulls, rams and lambs, with their grain offerings and their drink offerings and offer them on the altar of the house of your God which is in Jerusalem. [18] Whatever seems good to you and to your brothers to do with the rest of the silver and gold, you may do according to the will of your God. [19] Also the utensils which are given to you for the service of the house of your God, deliver in full before the God of Jerusalem. [20] The rest of the needs for the house of your God, for which you may have occasion to provide, provide *for it* from the royal treasury.

[21] "I, even I, King Artaxerxes, issue a decree to all the treasurers who are *in the provinces* beyond the River, that whatever Ezra the priest, the scribe of the law of the God of heaven, may require of you, it shall be done diligently, [22] *even* up to 100 talents of silver, 100 kors of wheat, 100 baths of wine, 100 baths of oil, and salt as needed. [23] Whatever is commanded by the God of heaven, let it be done with zeal for the house of the God of heaven, so that there will not be wrath against the kingdom of the king and his sons. [24] We also inform you that it is not allowed to impose tax, tribute or toll *on* any of the priests, Levites, singers, doorkeepers, Nethinim or servants of this house of God.

[25] "You, Ezra, according to the wisdom of your God which is in your hand, appoint magistrates and judges that they may judge all the people who are in *the province* beyond the River, *even* all those who know the laws of your God; and you may teach anyone who is ignorant *of them.* [26] Whoever will not observe the law of your God and the law of the king, let judgment be executed upon him strictly, whether for death or for banishment or for confiscation of goods or for imprisonment."

King Artaxerxes reveres the Lord. In these passages, he acknowledges Him as the God of heaven, Israel and Jerusalem. As God of heaven, He is in control of everything in the heavens and all that is controlled by, the time, weather and tide. By calling Him the God of Israel and Jerusalem, the king is admitting to the fact that even though they are under his authority, they are not his. This is quite humbling for a king to publicly say. He declares Him a living God, one with a will. He also calls him "your God," not his God. This knowledge gave him a reverential fear of God. He says, "So there will be no wrath against the kingdom of the king and his sons." King Artaxerxes is a righteous ruler, determined to keep his kingdom safe by putting himself and his people under the ban of the God of Israel.

King Artaxerxes was the king of Babylon. However, he revered Ezra, the priest and scribe of the Lord. He knew Ezra was learned in the commandments of the Lord. He not only allowed Ezra to go to Jerusalem to inquire of the Jews, but also released all of God's people, priests and Levites who were willing to go with him. He entrusted the silver and gold to Ezra.

He decreed to the treasurers of the provinces beyond the River to diligently do all that Ezra required of them. He decreed there would be no tax, tribute or toll imposed upon those whose work was in the service of the Temple at any level.

King Artaxerxes reveres the house of God. He did not send Ezra to Jerusalem empty-handed. He gave him the utensils for the Temple that were taken by King Nebuchadnezzar's army. He decreed that Ezra was to provide for the needs of the house of God out of the royal treasury. He commanded Ezra to buy bulls, rams and lambs with their grain and drink offerings to offer them on the altar of the house of God.

King Artaxerxes knows and reveres God's laws. He tells Ezra to appoint magistrates and judges who are living according to the laws of God, and to teach the laws to anyone who is ignorant of them. He declares that both the law of God and the law of the king to be the law of the land. There is to be strict judgment on those who will not observe them, even death.

King Artaxerxes was wise. He revered God and His laws so much that he implemented those laws into the laws of the land. In doing so, he set himself and his kingdom up for success and blessing. He also put a man of great integrity who was learned of the laws of God into a place of authority. This was his insurance that his dominion would please God and would not see His wrath.

Following is Ezra's response to the king's decree.

Ezra 7:27- 28

27 Blessed be the LORD, the God of our fathers, who has put *such a thing* as this in the king's heart, to adorn the house of the LORD which is in Jerusalem, 28 and has extended lovingkindness to me before the king and his counselors and before all the king's mighty princes. Thus I was strengthened according to the hand of the LORD my God upon me, and I gathered leading men from Israel to go up with me.

Ezra acknowledges that God was the One who made it all happen. The Lord was responsible for putting the desire into the king's heart to adorn His house in Jerusalem and revealed to the king, his counselors and his princes His love toward Ezra. Ezra understood his strength was according to the hand of the Lord his God which was upon him, so he gathered leading men from Israel to go with him.

Most of today's leaders fall short when it comes to knowledge of God and His laws. We have set ourselves up for failure. We have been deceived by continuously being told that a person's personal life and character should have nothing to do with their office in life. All we need to do is look back at history and see success and blessing upon the nations that implemented God's law into their own. We can also see the turmoil and poverty upon the nations that didn't. We are now witnessing firsthand what happens to successful nations when God's laws are removed. There is lawlessness, deception, chaos, immorality, division, unrest, turmoil and poverty. There is the lack of justice, honesty, order, purity, unity, peace, blessing and prosperity.

As King Artaxerxes did, we can choose to implement these laws back into our own. Over and over again, we see in the Old Testament various kings from Israel and Judah overturning these laws. They and the people inevitably paid dearly for it, and so will we. It is one thing not to know how to do things right. But to know and still choose to live in opposition to God is nothing but foolishness. It is truly challenging God's existence and can only bring His wrath upon the people. People in high places are accountable to God for their decisions and will be judged accordingly. We would be wise to learn from history.

Reverence to God is simply giving Him the respect and honor He deserves. It begins with obedience to His law. However, obedience is not a command, it is a choice.

God's law is summed up in the Ten Commandments. We need

to know and live by them. Then we will be blessed, regardless of what is happening around us. We need to teach them to the generations to come in order to protect them from the wrath of God. This is why our forefathers had them written in places of justice and learning. They wanted to make sure the generations to come would know and live by them. They were meant to be the standard of living. It is absolutely satanic to remove God and/or His laws from public places. Only Satan benefits when people are not taught God's laws. Reverence for God's law needs to be restored, if we want His blessings upon our nation.

We've seen how King Artaxerxes showed reverence to the Lord through his decree. Now, we will see how reverence was demonstrated in the New Testament and how we can show our reverence for Him to those in our lives.

Following is a question a Pharisee asked Jesus.

Matthew 22:36-40

³⁶ "Teacher, which is the great commandment in the Law?" ³⁷ And He said to him, "YOU SHALL LOVE THE LORD YOUR GOD WITH ALL YOUR HEART, AND WITH ALL YOUR SOUL, AND WITH ALL YOUR MIND.' ³⁸ This is the great and foremost commandment. ³⁹ The second is like it, 'YOU SHALL LOVE YOUR NEIGHBOR AS YOURSELF.' ⁴⁰ On these two commandments depend the whole Law and the Prophets."

The Ten Commandments are all about loving God and loving all people. Let's see what this looks like.

Colossians 3:12-17

¹² So, as those who have been chosen of God, holy and beloved, put on a heart of compassion, kindness, humility, gentleness and patience; ¹³ bearing with one another, and forgiving each other,

whoever has a complaint against anyone; just as the Lord forgave you, so also should you. [14] Beyond all these things *put on* love, which is the perfect bond of unity. [15] Let the peace of Christ rule in your hearts, to which indeed you were called in one body; and be thankful. [16] Let the word of Christ richly dwell within you, with all wisdom teaching and admonishing one another with psalms *and* hymns and spiritual songs, singing with thankfulness in your hearts to God. [17] Whatever you do in word or deed, *do* all in the name of the Lord Jesus, giving thanks through Him to God the Father.

We show reverence to the Lord when we, as His temple, bring honor to Him in our conduct. We should never forget God's grace and mercy when we or others fall short of His excellence. This is what He desires from us. We are not, nor will we ever be, perfect until we are with Him in heaven. Our love for people should exemplify His love for us.

II Peter 1:5-9

[5] Now for this very reason also, applying all diligence, in your faith supply moral excellence, and in *your* moral excellence, knowledge, [6] and in *your* knowledge, self-control, and in *your* self-control, perseverance, and in your perseverance, godliness, [7] and in *your* godliness, brotherly kindness, and in *your* brotherly kindness, love. [8] For if these *qualities* are yours and are increasing, they render you neither useless nor unfruitful in the true knowledge of our Lord Jesus Christ. [9] For he who lacks these *qualities* is blind *or* short-sighted, having forgotten *his* purification from his former sins.

When we revere the Lord, our love for Him and people will be worked out in our lives on a daily basis, moment by moment. Our reverence toward God gives us the desire to be more like Him. The changes in our own character will be seen. Moral excellence, knowledge, self-control, perseverance, godliness, brotherly kindness and love will increase.

Following is a passage Peter wrote regarding the written Word of God.

II Peter 3:1, 2

¹ This is now, beloved, the second letter I am writing to you in which I am stirring up your sincere mind by way of reminder, ² that you should remember the words spoken beforehand by the holy prophets and the commandment of the Lord and Savior *spoken* by your apostles.

Peter was reminding the church for a second time to remember the previously spoken words of the holy prophets, and the commandments of the Lord spoken by the apostles. He was referring to the books of prophecy in the Old Testament and to the words of the apostles, which are now the New Testament.

Matthew 5:17-19

¹⁷ "Do not think that I came to abolish the Law or the Prophets; I did not come to abolish but to fulfill. ¹⁸ For truly I say to you, until heaven and earth pass away, not the smallest letter or stroke shall pass from the Law until all is accomplished. ¹⁹ Whoever then annuls one of the least of these commandments, and teaches others *to do* the same, shall be called least in the kingdom of heaven; but whoever keeps and teaches *them*, he shall be called great in the kingdom of heaven.

Jesus is confirming the Law and the Prophets. We are to live by them. The difference now is that we have the abiding Holy Spirit that enables us to do so. This is what it means to die to self and live for the Lord. Total obedience shows reverence to the Lord. The Word of God is to be revered, none of it is obsolete. If you want to be great in the kingdom of heaven, you will keep and teach His commandments.

John 5:22—23

²² For not even the Father judges anyone, but He has given all judgment to the Son, ²³ so that all will honor the Son even as they honor the Father. He who does not honor the Son does not honor the Father who sent Him.

The Father has given all judgment to the Son. Why? So we would honor His Son as we honor Him. We show reverence to the Father when we revere the Son. Those who don't honor the Son don't honor the Father who sent Him. The Father was not happy with the way some treated His Son. This is His way of bringing honor to the Son for all that He went through: None shall come to the Father except through the Son.

John 7:14-18

¹⁴ But when it was now the midst of the feast Jesus went up into the temple, and *began* to teach. ¹⁵ The Jews then were astonished, saying, "How has this man become learned, having never been educated?" ¹⁶ So Jesus answered them and said, "My teaching is not Mine, but His who sent Me. ¹⁷ If anyone is willing to do His will, he will know of the teaching, whether it is of God or *whether* I speak from Myself. ¹⁸ He who speaks from himself seeks his own glory; but He who is seeking the glory of the One who sent Him, He is true, and there is no unrighteousness in Him.

Jesus reveres the Father. He gives Him all the glory. He exemplifies reverence. His teaching is God's teaching. In following His example, we would be wise not to speak from our own thoughts and ideas, giving our own opinions, seeking our own glory. When someone asks a question, determine to answer it with the truth. Make sure your teaching is not your own, but of the One who sent you. Jesus said. "Go and make disciples." This, too, is reverence.

John 10:16-18

[16] I have other sheep, which are not of this fold; I must bring them also, and they will hear My voice; and they will become one flock *with* one shepherd. [17] For this reason the Father loves Me, because I lay down My life so that I may take it again. [18] No one has taken it away from Me, but I lay it down on My own initiative. I have authority to lay it down, and I have authority to take it up again. This commandment I received from My Father."

Jesus is speaking of the gentiles, the sheep not of this fold. He is making it very clear that He came for them, as well as for Israel. We will know we are His because we will hear His voice. He must bring them into His flock so they become one. They will become one flock, the church. There will be One Shepherd, Jesus. This is why the Father loves Him, because He was willing to die and rise from the dead so all may be saved. No one took His life from Him. He freely gave it. He was given authority over life and death. He has the power to resurrect the dead. Because of what He did, we can now live with resurrection power. Because of this, we revere His voice and His every word.

Luke 10:39-42

[39] She had a sister called Mary, who was seated at the Lord's feet, listening to His word. [40] But Martha was distracted with all her preparations; and she came up to *Him* and said, "Lord, do You not care that my sister has left me to do all the serving alone? Then tell her to help me." [41] But the Lord answered and said to her, "Martha, Martha, you are worried and bothered about so many things; [42] but *only* one thing is necessary, for Mary has chosen the good part, which shall not be taken away from her."

We, too, would be wise to stop the busyness and chatter in our own lives. Mary chose the good part. She took time to sit at the Lord's feet and listen to His words. She showed reverence to the Son.

Jesus came so we could have life more abundantly. He deserves our reverence. You will see wherever you go people too busy to catch what is happening around them. Do yourself a favor and don't allow the world to steal your focus. Put your eyes upon Jesus and keep them there. He is in your midst. There is a lot going on in the spirit realm. We will see it when we quiet ourselves. Pray to Him to take off the blinders from your eyes so you can see as He sees. Ask Him to unstop your ears so you can hear as He hears. This is reverence. We are not our own. We were bought with His sacrificial blood.

We would be wise, as King Artaxerxes was, to once again give reverence and honor to God. This God of Israel is the same God who Jesus calls Father. He desires to be the Father of the nations. The choice is ours. He is worthy of our reverence.

Holy, Holy, Holy

Holy, Holy, Holy, Lord God Almighty!
Early in the morning our song shall rise to Thee:
Holy, Holy, Holy! Merciful and Mighty!
God in Three Persons, blessed Trinity!

Holy, Holy, Holy! All the saints adore Thee,
Casting down their golden crowns around the glassy sea;
Cherubim and seraphim falling down before Thee,
Who wert, and art, and evermore shalt be.

Holy, Holy, Holy! Tho' the darkness hide Thee,
Tho' the eye of sinful man Thy glory may not see,
Only Thou art Holy; there is none beside Thee
Perfect in pow'r, in love, and purity.

Holy, Holy, Holy! Lord God Almighty!
All Thy works shall praise Thy name in earth and sky and sea;
Holy, Holy, Holy! Merciful and Mighty!
God in Three Persons, blessed Trinity! Amen.

Written by: Reginald Heber

DAY 15

SERVICE

Service: the work performed by one that serves;
help, use, benefit; contribution to the welfare of others.
Serve: to be a servant; to be of use;
to give the service and respect due; attend;
Attend: to be ready for service; to be present.

This week, we are going to gain understanding on how to grow in our walk with Christ. Service is a vital part of the Christian life. We are here to serve the Lord by serving others for His glory. Those we are serving will see Christ in us, when we are serving in the place we are supposed to be. It will be Him, using us as empty vessels. We'll see that God did not leave us without instruction for leadership. We are going to see the who, what, when, where and why of service. We'll begin by taking a closer look at those serving with Ezra.

Ezra 8:1

¹ Now these are the heads of their fathers' households and the genealogical enrollment of those who went up with me from Babylon in the reign of King Artaxerxes:

The names and genealogy of those who went to Jerusalem with Ezra are written in the first fourteen verses of Chapter 8. There were well over a thousand men with Ezra. However, when they assembled at the river, Ezra observed them and found none from the family of Levi.

Ezra 8:15-20

15 Now I assembled them at the river that runs to Ahava, where we camped for three days; and when I observed the people and the priests, I did not find any Levites there. 16 So I sent for Eliezer, Ariel, Shemaiah, Elnathan, Jarib, Elnathan, Nathan, Zechariah and Meshullam, leading men, and for Joiarib and Elnathan, teachers. 17 I sent them to Iddo the leading man at the place Casiphia; and I told them what to say to Iddo *and* his brothers, the temple servants at the place Casiphia, *that is*, to bring ministers to us for the house of our God. 18 According to the good hand of our God upon us they brought us a man of insight of the sons of Mahli, the son of Levi, the son of Israel, namely Sherebiah, and his sons and brothers, 18 men; 19 and Hashabiah and Jeshaiah of the sons of Merari, with his brothers and their sons, 20 men; 20 and 220 of the temple servants, whom David and the princes had given for the service of the Levites, all of them designated by name.

Ezra had wisdom, knowledge and understanding of the Word of God. That is how he knew that only Levites were authorized by God to carry out certain tasks. He wisely observed those with him and noted there were no Levites. He sent leading men to Casiphia to bring Levites to them for the house of God. Ezra didn't tell them who to bring. He trusted God to hand pick, through Iddo and his brothers, those who were to serve in Israel. God was faithful. They brought Sherebiah, a man of insight, with his sons and brothers, Hashabiah, and Jeshaiah with his sons and brothers. There were thirty-eight Levites and two hundred twenty servants. All of them were designated by name. During the seventy years of captivity, these men were prepared to one day serve in the Temple. They were prepared and ready. This was their call in life.

Ezra 8:32-33

³² Thus we came to Jerusalem and remained there three days.

³³ On the fourth day the silver and the gold and the utensils were weighed out in the house of our God into the hand of Meremoth the son of Uriah the priest, and with him *was* Eleazar the son of Phinehas; and with them *were* the Levites, Jozabad the son of Jeshua and Noadiah the son of Binnui.

They remained in Jerusalem three days before they did anything with the silver, gold and utensils they had brought. Ezra was observing those serving in the Temple. This three-day period was not only for rest but also for discernment. He had silver and gold to deliver for the king and his counselors, as an offering to the God of Israel. He was not about to put it into the wrong hands. These items were weighed when they were given to the Levites at the river. They were weighed again, in Jerusalem, as they were given to Meremoth (who had Eleazar with him), in front of Jozabad and Noadiah, the Levites.

Ezra 8:35

³⁵ The exiles who had come from the captivity offered burnt offerings to the God of Israel: 12 bulls for all Israel, 96 rams, 77 lambs, 12 male goats for a sin offering, all as a burnt offering to the LORD.

They are offered on the altar to the God of Israel the bulls, rams and lambs the king ordered them to buy with the silver and gold. They also offered twelve male goats for a sin offering. They were not only serving God and His people, but they were also serving the king for the good of his kingdom. Notice that they did not deviate from their orders. They were obedient in their service.

Ezra 8:36

36 Then they delivered the king's edicts to the king's satraps and to the governors *in the provinces* beyond the River, and they supported the people and the house of God.

Remember that the king's edict was in support of the Jews, not the satraps and governors. This edict ordered the treasurers to supply for Ezra's every need. The edict gave Ezra the authority to appoint magistrates and judges the authority to judge all the people who were in the province.

Ezra is a godly example of a servant worthy to be followed. He took care of God's business first, and then he took care of the king's. He served according to God's design. He fasted and prayed before placing anything into anyone's hands. He made sure those in service were serving in the capacity in which they were authorized by God to serve. They did what was spelled out to them by God through Moses. These laws were to be strictly followed. Ezra was favored because he knew and took his calling very seriously.

Let's take a look at another example of a righteous servant worthy to be followed.

John 13:3-8

3 *Jesus*, knowing that the Father had given all things into His hands, and that He had come forth from God and was going back to God, 4 *got up from supper, and *laid aside His garments; and taking a towel, He girded Himself.

5 Then He *poured water into the basin, and began to wash the disciples' feet and to wipe them with the towel with which He was girded. 6 So He *came to Simon Peter. He *said to Him, "Lord, do You wash my feet?" 7 Jesus answered and said to him, "What I do you do not realize now, but you will understand hereafter." 8 Peter

*said to Him, "Never shall You wash my feet!" Jesus answered him, "If I do not wash you, you have no part with Me."**

Jesus, the Messiah, washed the feet of the disciples, so who are we to think we are too good for such work? Serving others is the most gratifying work we can ever do. Unfortunately, however, we often allow our pride to keep us from the Lord's best.

The spiritual aspect of this story is that we have to be washed by Jesus if we want to have any part of Him. This is the first credential for serving Him. We must be washed in His blood, by accepting Him as Lord and Savior.

Ezra made sure he placed in service those whom the Lord had chosen, specifically the Levites. We, the church, also have biblical guidelines to follow. Let's read the qualifications for overseers and deacons.

I Timothy 3:1-13

[1] It is a trustworthy statement: if any man aspires to the office of overseer, it is a fine work he desires *to do*. [2] An overseer, then, must be above reproach, the husband of one wife, temperate, prudent, respectable, hospitable, able to teach, [3] not addicted to wine or pugnacious, but gentle, peaceable, free from the love of money. [4] *He must* be one who manages his own household well, keeping his children under control with all dignity [5] (but if a man does not know how to manage his own household, how will he take care of the church of God?), [6] *and* not a new convert, so that he will not become conceited and fall into the condemnation incurred by the devil. [7] And he must have a good reputation with those outside *the church*, so that he will not fall into reproach and the snare of the devil.

[8] Deacons likewise *must be* men of dignity, not double-tongued, or addicted to much wine or fond of sordid gain, [9] *but* holding to the

**mystery of the faith with a clear conscience. ¹⁰ These men must also
first be tested; then let them serve as deacons if they are beyond
reproach. ¹¹ Women *must* likewise be dignified, not malicious
gossips, but temperate, faithful in all things. ¹² Deacons must be
husbands of *only* one wife, and good managers of *their* children and
their own households. ¹³ For those who have served well as deacons
obtain for themselves a high standing and great confidence in the
faith that is in Christ Jesus.**

The Lord leaves no room for mistake. He is very clear regarding
these qualifications. Overseers and Deacons must be proven to be of
godly character and above reproach. Their lives are to be lived as an
open book. They must not be double-tongued, saying one thing to
one person or group and something else to another. They are not
to be alcoholics or fond of sordid gain. An overseer must be able to
control his temper and be prudent. He must also be able to teach
and be free from the love of money. His household must be well
managed and his children under control with all dignity. He must be
a man of one wife. Women must be dignified, not malicious gossips
or hot tempered, and they must be faithful in all things.

We prepare ourselves for service by becoming more like Jesus
every day. He will open doors for us.

Proverbs 3:5-6

**⁵ Trust in the LORD with all your heart
And do not lean on your own understanding.**

**⁶ In all your ways acknowledge Him,
And He will make your paths straight.**

The Lord is cleansing His house of those who don't qualify
for the positions they hold. We don't have the right to challenge,
let alone change, God's Word. We have to trust that He knows
what He is doing. There is a lot of work to be done. If you are in a

position you are not qualified for, then you are hindering someone from fulfilling the position meant for them. On the other hand, if you are qualified for a position that needs to be filled, step up to the plate and let the church decide if you are the right person or not. There are positions specifically for elders and elders alone. The word elder means an older person. We do not retire in the church body.

Titus 2:1-10

¹ But as for you, speak the things which are fitting for sound doctrine. ² Older men are to be temperate, dignified, sensible, sound in faith, in love, in perseverance.

³ Older women likewise are to be reverent in their behavior, not malicious gossips nor enslaved to much wine, teaching what is good, ⁴ so that they may encourage the young women to love their husbands, to love their children, ⁵ *to be* sensible, pure, workers at home, kind, being subject to their own husbands, so that the word of God will not be dishonored.

⁶ Likewise urge the young men to be sensible; ⁷ in all things show yourself to be an example of good deeds, *with* purity in doctrine, dignified, ⁸ sound *in* speech which is beyond reproach, so that the opponent will be put to shame, having nothing bad to say about us.

⁹ *Urge* bondslaves to be subject to their own masters in everything, to be well-pleasing, not argumentative, ¹⁰ not pilfering, but showing all good faith so that they will adorn the doctrine of God our Savior in every respect.

We were designed, before the beginning of time, for such a time as this. We need to take responsibility for the way we serve the people with whom the Lord has blessed us. We are to be the light of the world through the indwelling Holy Spirit, just as Jesus was. We are here to serve others and make their lives better. Then, the Lord will give us the desires of our heart. We are not to be self-serving.

James 3:1

¹ Let not many *of you* become teachers, my brethren, knowing that as such we will incur a stricter judgment.

This passage scared me. I already felt unworthy of the forgiveness I had received. I certainly didn't want to put myself in a place where stricter judgment would incur. Therefore, when I was first asked to teach, I declined. Afterwards, the Lord clearly spoke to me, saying He would lead and guide me and would keep me from falling into temptation, and I was not to worry. He assured me that I would be fine. I then called the person back and agreed to accept the position, acknowledging that it was the Lord's will. The Lord, so to speak, reeled me back in when I was heading down the wrong path. That was the picture He had given me. He is faithful. We can count on Him. That is why He is going to hold us accountable for the things He has asked of us.

Be at peace. Go through the doors he opens for you and let all things happen in His perfect timing. Then you will know that you are ready and in His perfect will. He will lead and guide you. He will protect you from falling if you stay in close contact with Him. Let it be all of Him and none of you. Surrender to Him, He is the Author and Finisher. He will complete the good work He began in you.

God is a God of order. He is to be first in our life. Our spouse is second, our children are third, and then comes work and the church. When we put God first, He is with us in the rest. This is the secret to a fulfilled and happy life. Never put your children before your spouse. They are yours only for a brief time, then will go out and start a life of their own. How well they are able to do this depends upon the example you give them. We are not to allow our jobs to come before our families or the Lord. Work is not to be our life; its purpose is to support our life. When we serve those whom the Lord has placed in our lives, we can trust Him to take care of our needs in return. This is a spiritual law and an awesome promise that we can stand on; it must happen. When you maintain this order, you can trust that you are in the Lord's will.

When we hire someone to care for our loved ones, we are responsible for making sure they live by the same value system we do. We need to make sure everyone is building on the same foundation.

When we serve the Lord, we are to be completely yielded to Him, empty vessels for His glory. It should be Him that others see and hear. We need to be open to what He calls us to do. Pray for Him to open a door of service for you. When He does, step in, and expect Him to bless your efforts and obedience. We too often think that we should be doing what comes natural for us. This is not necessarily true. For me, it has most often been the opposite. I have found myself doing things I could never do without the Lord's indwelling Spirit. The Bible says our weakness shall become our strength. The only way this happens is if we step out of our comfort zone, and do that which the Lord has put before us. He is Faithful and True. He will never ask you to do something without empowering you for the task. So step out in faith and just do it.

Sometimes, we allow our pride to get in the way of our service, believing that we are above what someone has asked us to help with. I have time and time again heard people say they won't help in the children's ministry, because they aren't good with kids, when this is the one thing continually requested of them. That is disobedience. We do not jump over hurdles in the ministry. The Lord knows what we need to do, before we are ready to move on to something else. Quite often, we think the parents of young children are those who should be serving in the children's ministry, when what these parents need is some time with adults. Young parents need to be in a class where they are being fed the Word of God to help them become the parents they desire to be. Parenting is tough work.

We are to be the best we can possibly be to everyone the Lord puts on our path and serve them all with a joyful heart. Remember the promises you made to make your spouse and children your number-one priority. They are God's blessing to you, and you will be held accountable for the way you serve them. The Holy Spirit is with you to lead and guide you. When you are frustrated, separate yourself from the situation for a moment and seek His help. This is His desire.

Matthew 25:21

21 "His master said to him, 'Well done, good and faithful slave. You were faithful with a few things, I will put you in charge of many things; enter into the joy of your master.'

We all want to hear, "Well done, good and faithful servant." The Lord will place you where you are supposed to be. Be faithful with the things He has entrusted to you, and He will put you in charge of much more. Enter into the joy of your Master.

O For a Thousand Tongues to Sing

O for a thousand tongues to sing
My great Redeemer's praise,
The glories of my God and King,
The triumphs of His grace!

My gracious Master and my God,
Assist me to proclaim,
To spread through all the earth abroad
The honors of Thy name.

Jesus! the name that charms our fears,
That bids our sorrows cease;
'Tis music in the sinner's ears,
'Tis life, and health, and peace.

He breaks the power of canceled sin,
He sets the prisoner free;
His blood can make the foulest clean,
His blood availed for me.

Written by: Charles Wesley

DAY 16

FASTING

Fast: to abstain from food:
to eat sparingly or abstain from some foods;

Abstain: to refrain deliberately and often with an effort of self-denial
from an action or practice.

Yesterday, we looked at service.   Today, we'll look at the importance and purpose of fasting.   We'll go back to the place at the river where Ezra and those with him were assembled.   We'll observe what they did while they were there.

Ezra 8:21-22

21 Then I proclaimed a fast there at the river of Ahava, that we might humble ourselves before our God to seek from Him a safe journey for us, our little ones, and all our possessions. 22 For I was ashamed to request from the king troops and horsemen to protect us from the enemy on the way, because we had said to the king, "The hand of our God is favorably disposed to all those who seek Him, but His power and His anger are against all those who forsake Him."

Ezra proclaimed a fast. They were to humble themselves before God to seek from Him a safe journey. These men were not traveling alone. They had precious cargo. They had their families, all that the king gave them for the Temple and livestock. This was a huge procession and was wide open for ambush. They knew they had enemies, especially in the province they were about to enter.

Because they had boasted to the king regarding the Lord's protection and favor on those who seek Him, they were ashamed to ask him for protection. Ezra showed wisdom by seeking safety from the Lord. He did not assume God would keep them safe. Ezra needed to know he had God's protection. Therefore, he proclaimed a fast.

There are those today who believe God is there for others, but don't trust Him for themselves. Here, we learn from Ezra's example that we fast in order to know that God's hand is favorably disposed to us. Then we can trust God to be faithful to us in the things He has promised. God honors fasting; it is a form of humility.

Ezra 8:23, 31

²³ So we fasted and sought our God concerning this *matter*, and He listened to our entreaty.

³¹ Then we journeyed from the river Ahava on the twelfth of the first month to go to Jerusalem; and the hand of our God was over us, and He delivered us from the hand of the enemy and the ambushes by the way.

Ezra said God listened to their entreaty. He knew this because the peace of the Lord must have fallen upon them. When peace falls upon us, we know the Lord is with us and has heard our petition. After they sought God and He listened to their entreaty, Ezra and those with him journeyed to Jerusalem in peace.

Remember, God's desire is that we seek Him in all things. Fasting shows the Lord that we are so determined to hear from Him that we will abstain from food until we do. The purpose of fasting is to give our undivided attention to the Lord for an answer to our entreaty. Instead of eating, we get our nourishment from the Word of God. The more we seek the Lord during a fast, the less hungry we feel. After a few days, the hunger diminishes.

Ezra and those with him fasted for their safety. No matter what your purpose is, fasting is a wonderful way to become more intimate with God and to hear His voice. Be obedient to the call on your life and seek the Lord daily. Take your responsibility for those He has placed in your life seriously and fast for them, if needed.

Queen Esther also called the Jews in Susa to a three-day fast for her safety.

Esther 4:16

¹⁶ "Go, assemble all the Jews who are found in Susa, and fast for me; do not eat or drink for three days, night or day. I and my maidens also will fast in the same way. And thus I will go in to the king, which is not according to the law; and if I perish, I perish."

With the king's permission, Haman, the king's right-hand man, wrote an edict that on a certain day the people were allowed to kill all of the Jews. Queen Esther was a Jew. Her husband, the king of Persia, was not aware of this. She needed to tell him that if Haman's plan was to succeed, she too would be killed. The lives of her people were at stake. However, it was unlawful for anyone to go before the king without a summons. He could put her to death for not adhering to protocol. By going before him without a summons, she would be putting her life in her own hands. By proclaiming a fast, however, she was taking it out of her hands and putting it into God's. She fully trusted God to honor the fast. She stood by her people. She knew that she was the queen of Persia "for such a time as this." Her fast was successful and the king made an edict to protect the Jews. Haman was hung, along with his sons.

Fasting is a powerful tool that we have which helps us to draw closer to God. It tells God we trust Him with our lives and are putting them in His hands. We are telling God we know He is able to turn our situation for the better. It was not Queen Esther that saved the people, it was God. He gave Esther favor before the king. He revealed to the king what needed to be done to turn this edict around. He turned what their enemy meant for evil into good.

Following is a picture of Israel in a desolate state. Imagine looking at a field and seeing this.

Joel 1:4

⁴ What the gnawing locust has left, the swarming locust has eaten; And what the swarming locust has left, the creeping locust has eaten; And what the creeping locust has left, the stripping locust has eaten.

There was literally nothing left. They were at their end. Then, God sent the prophet Joel to the elders and people of Israel. As is in every case, complacency toward God was the cause of the desolation, of His people. Joel was to tell them how to break this complacency and restore their faith.

Joel 2:15-17

¹⁵ Blow a trumpet in Zion,
    Consecrate a fast, proclaim a solemn assembly,

¹⁶ Gather the people, sanctify the congregation,
    Assemble the elders,
    Gather the children and the nursing infants.
    Let the bridegroom come out of his room
    And the bride out of her *bridal* chamber.

¹⁷ Let the priests, the LORD'S ministers,
>   Weep between the porch and the altar,
>   And let them say, "Spare Your people, O LORD,
>   And do not make Your inheritance a reproach,
>   A byword among the nations.
>   Why should they among the peoples say,
>   'Where is their God?'"

They were to blow a trumpet, signifying war. This was going to be a spiritual war. It would be won through fasting and prayer. It would destroy the complacency of God's people and bring them back to right standing with Him. It would also usher in restoration. The purpose of this fast was to humbly cry out to the Lord for His mercy and help. They were hopeless without Him. He told them to weep and ask Him to spare His people. They were to seek the Lord, the bridegroom, for restoration. The Lord did not nor would He ever call a fast if He weren't going to honor it.

Joel 2:18-19

¹⁸ Then the LORD will be zealous for His land
>   And will have pity on His people.

¹⁹ The LORD will answer and say to His people,
>   "Behold, I am going to send you grain, new wine and oil,
>   And you will be satisfied in full with them;
>   And I will never again make you a reproach among the
>   nations.

He promises to be zealous for the land and to have pity on His people. He responds as their Provider, promising to send grain, new wine and oil. He will send enough that they will be satisfied in full with them. He responds as Deliverer, saying He will never again make them a reproach among the nations. This is a day coming, for we know Israel is currently a reproach among many nations.

A solemn assembly is a holy summons to meet together. That is all we can do when our situation is too big for us to handle. The rest is up to the Lord. His hands are tied, until we loosen them, by crying out to Him and asking Him for help. He will not take anything from us. We have to willfully give Him all that concerns us. Unfortunately, our natural tendency is to try to take care of our problems by ourselves. This is not now nor has it ever been God's plan or desire. He wants to be involved in everything we do.

Throughout the world today, we see property and stock values deteriorating, retirement plans vanishing, wages dropping, jobs disappearing, taxes consuming earnings, government spending increasing and, at the same time, the cost of food rising.

It is important for us to never forget the Lord is with us and wants to help us at all times. He is our Provider and Deliverer. When things seem to be out of control, consecrate a fast, gather a solemn assembly and cry out to the Lord. He loves it when His church is united in fasting and prayer. Cry out to the Lover of your soul. He loves you! Nothing is impossible for God. He is the God of restoration.

God is always there for us. Sometimes, we get so wrapped up in the little things of life that we miss the big picture. Before we know it, everything seems to be caving in on us all at once. Then we realize our mistake. We depended way too much upon our own intellect rather than upon God's wisdom. The result is that we feel devastated and hopeless.

There is good news, however. It is never too late to seek the Lord. He is the God of restoration. It doesn't matter if the desolation we find ourselves in is personal or national, God can handle it. Nothing catches Him by surprise or is too big for Him to handle. When we feel devastated and hopeless, we would be wise to call a solemn fast. This is a practice that is almost unheard of today, because we, the church, have become so tolerant we don't want to offend anyone by putting demands on them. So, instead, we allow the destruction around us to continue. We need to come out of our comfort zone, take a step in faith and call a solemn fast. Then we will see God in action.

Now, let's see what the New Testament has to say about fasting.

Matthew 4:1-2

¹ Then Jesus was led up by the Spirit into the wilderness to be tempted by the devil. ² And after He had fasted forty days and forty nights, He then became hungry.

This took place right after Jesus was baptized by John the Baptist. He was led by the Holy Spirit into the wilderness to be tempted by the devil. Temptation always follows a good decision. Fasting during the time of temptation strengthens us, since it draws us closer to the Lord. Jesus fasted for forty days and nights then became hungry.

Jesus was led by the Holy Spirit. A fast is only beneficial if it is led by the Lord. Don't fast to appear godly. Fast to hear from the Lord. If peace isn't present or if hunger never subsides, then quit and assume it is not the Lord's will. I have had successful and unsuccessful fasts and have determined that success is based upon who called the fast. Did I call the fast, was it someone else or was it the Lord? Just because someone else is fasting doesn't mean we are to join them. However, don't be too quick to dismiss it either. Pray about it. The Lord knows the future and if the timing is right for you to be fasting. He may have a plan for you that includes eating. If you are in the middle of a fast, you'll miss the opportunity.

It is exciting when the Lord calls a fast, because we know we are going to hear from Him one way or another and that He's going to give us divine wisdom, knowledge and understanding. When we fast, He opens our eyes and ears to see and hear as He does. We can expect to have visions and receive clear direction during a fast. Visions can appear as thoughts or daydreams. Often, they are promises to get us, or the one we are fasting for, through hard times ahead. Whatever they are, you can be sure they will come to pass if you do what the Lord asks you to do. Remember, when you are seeking the Lord's will, He will show it to you. Then it is up to you to be obedient.

Fasting should be a peaceful time and also an exciting time. This only happens when it is led by the Holy Spirit. During your fast, you should have the energy you need to do what has to be done. If you don't, then stop and wait for another time. You should separate yourself from activities that aren't a must. Set this time aside for the Lord; it is to be holy.

When Satan tempted Jesus, Jesus answered him by quoting the Word of God to him. This is how we fight the enemy as well. We are able to withstand him when we know the Word of God.

After forty days of fasting in the wilderness, Jesus became hungry. This is the scripture I use in order to know when my fast is over. When I get hungry, I eat. This usually happens after 3, 7, 10, 21 or 40 days.

Let's see what Jesus did after His fast.

Matthew 4:17

¹⁷ From that time Jesus began to preach and say, "Repent, for the kingdom of heaven is at hand."

Jesus' baptism and forty days of fasting and temptation preceded the launching of His ministry. After that, He began to preach.

A forty-day fast is often used to usher in the beginning of a ministry. During such a fast, make sure you remain hydrated and keep your salt and sugar levels up as needed. I allow myself to drink small quantities of chicken broth and diluted juice. The chicken broth helps me when I am feeling light-headed or out of sorts. The juice helps when I find myself getting agitated. Do not do this unless you are positive the Lord has called you to such a fast. We do not use fasting as a weight-loss solution. It is for spiritual purposes only. Trust the Holy Spirit to lead and guide you as He did with Jesus.

Fasting can also bring us to a new level in our walk with God. It proves to Him that we are willing to give up the lusts of the world in order to serve Him better. Being a form of humility, fasting tells the Lord we are desperately in need of Him and are not willing to walk without Him. Moses said he was not willing to go if God wasn't going with him. This should be our heart's desire, as well. Time is too valuable to make unnecessary mistakes when the Lord is at our side, waiting for us to come to Him for guidance and encouragement.

Be careful not to push what you are called to do onto others. We all have our own call. Don't worry about what everyone else is doing. Instead, be happy that the Lord has chosen you to fast for His purposes. Let's see what Jesus had to say to those who worried about what others were doing.

Luke 5:33

33 And they said to Him, "The disciples of John often fast and offer prayers, the *disciples* of the Pharisees also do the same, but Yours eat and drink."

They were upset because Jesus' disciples were not fasting like they thought they should be.

Luke 5:34

34 And Jesus said to them, "You cannot make the attendants of the

bridegroom fast while the bridegroom is with them, can you?

Jesus is the bridegroom. The disciples are His attendants. The church is His betrothed. He will one day return for her and there will be a wedding feast. Jesus was saying there are times to fast and times to celebrate. In this case, they were celebrating His Presence among them. After He was gone, they would have plenty of time for fasting.

God is a God of order and blessing. We cannot win people to Christ if we are dogmatic in our ways. Remember the priorities in your life and make sure that you are not putting fasting or anything else before them. I would not fast if the timing would keep me from being a blessing to someone else or from celebrating with someone I should celebrate with. God is the Author of feasts and celebrations. I do not believe He would call us to fast during such a time.

Following are some instructions for fasting.

Matthew 6:16-18

16 "Whenever you fast, do not put on a gloomy face as the hypocrites *do*, for they neglect their appearance so that they will be noticed by men when they are fasting. Truly I say to you, they have their reward in full. 17 But you, when you fast, anoint your head and wash your face 18 so that your fasting will not be noticed by men, but by your Father who is in secret; and your Father who sees *what is done* in secret will reward you.

When we fast, we should not bring attention to ourselves. Our fasting is to be kept between us, the Lord and those called to fast with us.

Fasting helps us to separate ourselves from the world so we can give the Lord our undivided attention. During this time, we will hear from Him. However, when He speaks He wants us to hear Him out. He wants our undivided attention. Give it to Him. Fasting will bring you closer to God than you have ever been before. Fast and see that the Lord is Faithful and True. He is our Provider and Deliverer. Let fasting become a part of your spiritual walk. It has been neglected for far too long. Be blessed.

Open My Eyes, That I May See

Open my eyes, that I may see
Glimpses of truth Thou hast for me;
Place in my hands the wonderful key
That shall unclasp and set me free.

Refrain

Silently now I wait for Thee,
Ready my God, Thy will to see,
Open my eyes, illumine me,
Spirit divine!

Open my ears, that I may hear
Voices of truth Thou sendest clear;
And while the wave notes fall on my ear,
Everything false will disappear.

Refrain

Open my mouth, and let me bear,
Gladly the warm truth everywhere;
Open my heart and let me prepare
Love with Thy children thus to share.

Refrain

Written by: Clara H. Scott

DAY 17

ACCOUNTABILITY

Accountability: the quality or state of being accountable;
an obligation or willingness to accept responsibility
or to account for one's actions.
Accountable: subject to giving an account;
capable of being accounted for.
Responsible: liable to be called on to answer;
able to answer for one's conduct and obligations.
Trustworthy: able to choose for oneself between right and wrong.

Accountability is a must; if we want the Lord to restore what has been lost or taken from us along the way. We cannot expect the Lord to bless us, if we are not willing to hold ourselves accountable for what we already have and know. Remember, we're not in this alone. He gave us the Holy Spirit who will reveal to us right from wrong. When He does, we are to do what is right. This is being accountable for what we know. This is being accountable for what we do.

We are going to look at what Ezra did, after the fast, while with the assembly at the river. We will learn how to make sure those we entrust our treasures to, realize they will be held accountable for them.

Ezra 8:24

²⁴ Then I set apart twelve of the leading priests, Sherebiah, Hashabiah, and with them ten of their brothers;

These priests were twelve of the Levites that came from Casiphia. Sherebiah was the Levite who Ezra said was a man of insight. This meant he heard from God. He knew God's voice and was given dreams, visions, revelations, etc... When Sherebiah heard from the Lord, he held himself accountable for what he heard. Insight comes with a reverential fear of the Lord, as well as a determination to do all that He reveals to us, in order to see the vision fulfilled. Therefore, Sherebiah was a great choice for a position in which accountability was of utmost importance.

Let's see what service Ezra set these twelve men apart for.

Ezra 8:25-27

²⁵ and I weighed out to them the silver, the gold and the utensils, the offering for the house of our God which the king and his counselors and his princes and all Israel present *there* had offered. ²⁶ Thus I weighed into their hands 650 talents of silver, and silver utensils *worth* 100 talents, *and* 100 gold talents, ²⁷ and 20 gold bowls *worth* 1,000 darics, and two utensils of fine shiny bronze, precious as gold.

Ezra knew these men were trustworthy. This was confirmed to him during the fast. Therefore, he entrusted them with the silver, the gold and the utensils that had been entrusted to him by the king. This wasn't something Ezra took lightly. The offering was huge and irreplaceable. His reputation as a man of God was at stake, and he took his responsibilities seriously. Because he was trustworthy, he was favored by God, the king, and all those with him. Notice how Ezra personally weighed out everything. This way, everyone knew exactly what they were accountable for, and the temptation to steal was removed. In other words, greed wasn't given an opportunity to come in, let alone flourish.

Ezra 8:28-29

28 Then I said to them, "You are holy to the LORD, and the utensils are holy; and the silver and the gold are a freewill offering to the LORD God of your fathers. 29 Watch and keep *them* until you weigh *them* before the leading priests, the Levites and the heads of the fathers' households of Israel at Jerusalem, *in* the chambers of the house of the LORD."

Notice that the priests and the utensils were holy. The silver and gold weren't. Ezra said this to remind them that they and the utensils were designed by God and made specifically for His purposes. This is what made them holy. They were created by God in order to serve Him.

Ezra gave them clear instructions. They were to watch and keep everything given to them safe until they personally weighed it all before the leading priests, the Levites and the heads of the father's households of Israel. This way, *everyone* knew *everything* weighed in at the proper weight and that *nothing* was missing. The weighing was to take place in the chambers of the Temple, in Jerusalem.

Five months later, on the first day of the fifth month, they arrived in Jerusalem.

Ezra 8:33-36

33 On the fourth day the silver and the gold and the utensils were weighed out in the house of our God into the hand of Meremoth the son of Uriah the priest, and with him *was* Eleazar the son of Phinehas; and with them *were* the Levites, Jozabad the son of Jeshua and Noadiah the son of Binnui. 34 Everything was numbered and weighed, and all the weight was recorded at that time.

³⁵ **The exiles who had come from the captivity offered burnt offerings to the God of Israel: 12 bulls for all Israel, 96 rams, 77 lambs, 12 male goats for a sin offering, all as a burnt offering to the LORD.** ³⁶ **Then they delivered the king's edicts to the king's satraps and to the governors** *in the provinces* **beyond the River, and they supported the people and the house of God.**

The twelve men Ezra chose kept all that was given to them safe. Four days after arriving in Jerusalem, they weighed it into the hand of Meremoth, a priest. With him were Levites and Eleazar, the son of Phinehas, who represented the heads of the fathers of Israel. Everyone who was to be present was there, and everything was accounted for. First, they offered the burnt offerings to the God of Israel. Then they delivered the king's edict to the satraps and governors and supported the people and house of God. They did everything they set out to do. They did not tarry, but did everything in a timely manner.

Ezra was under the king's authority. He was given this incredible opportunity because he was a man of integrity. He was a man who could be trusted with great treasures and responsibilities. He took responsibility for his own actions and the actions of all those under his authority.

We, too, need to be wise like the king, and make certain that those we place in positions of authority are of good character and reputation. Unfortunately, we have placed ungodly men and women in places of great authority and are seeing the consequences of it. We are watching countries fail because of ungodly leaders. There seems to be no one taking responsibility for anyone or anything. We live in a time of lawlessness. There is financial devastation because regulations were removed, enabling those in authority to do whatever they wanted. They sacrificed the wealth of those they represent for their own sordid gain.

This is not the kind of sacrifice that is acceptable in God's eyes. Greed has overcome those in authority. Instead of being held accountable, they are being bailed out. This is an atrocity. When the consequences of poor choices catch up with us, we need to take responsibility for them. This should be a time of humility. The Lord gives favor to those who choose to humble themselves. It is pride that competes with humility. It is pride that goes before the fall. Sooner or later, the consequences will be paid for, hopefully by those responsible for them and not their victims or children.

When we choose to take responsibility for our actions, it pleases the Lord far beyond His anger. He doesn't care about what we did yesterday. He cares about what we choose to do today. If you have wronged someone through poor choices, do yourself a favor by confessing and asking the Lord for forgiveness. Then, He will smile upon you and help you beyond what you can imagine. He is a loving and forgiving God. He is waiting for His people to humble themselves and call upon Him. He is ready to help. He is the God of restoration!

We now know the importance of taking into consideration the character of those we place into positions of authority. Jesus said, "Follow Me." He is our perfect example. We are to be imitators of Jesus. No matter where we find ourselves, all we need to ever ask ourselves is, what would Jesus do? Therein lies the answer to every situation. This is the key to a life of integrity. Walk with the insight of the Lord. Walk in reverence to our Lord and King. Ezra took his responsibility to the king seriously. We need to take our responsibility to the King of Kings seriously. We will be brought before Him. We will give an accounting for all that He gave us.

Let's see what the Bible says about righteousness and justice.

Proverbs 8:20-21

20 "I walk in the way of righteousness,

In the midst of the paths of justice,

**²¹ To endow those who love me with wealth,
That I may fill their treasuries.**

This is a wonderful picture of Jesus walking in the midst of those who are living righteously and justly. He is watching us. When we are living the life that glorifies Him and His ways, He will bless us, in this case with wealth. This means when a nation finds itself financially unstable, it would be wise to consider the possibility that it has not acted righteously or justly, and that corruption has been allowed to creep in.

Just as Ezra carefully chose those who would serve with him, we were also carefully chosen. Jesus chose us and entrusted His treasure to us. This treasure is the good news that He came to save the lost, so we could have eternal life and live with Him and the Father in heaven. He did not abandon us. He gave us His indwelling Holy Spirit to lead and guide us along the path of righteousness and justice. The world is full of hurting, lost and deceived people ready to hear the good news. Be bold in the Spirit and tell them about your Jesus. We will give an accounting to Him regarding this great treasure He entrusted to us.

John 14:6

⁶ Jesus *said to him, "I am the way, and the truth, and the life; no one comes to the Father but through Me.

This is our King's edict. We are to deliver it to the world.

Ezra's 12 chosen men also supported God's people and His house. We will be held accountable for doing the same. We are to support God's people by loving one another.

John 13:34-35

³⁴ "A new commandment I give to you, that you love one another,

even as I have loved you, that you also love one another. **³⁵ By this all men will know that you are My disciples, if you have love for one another."**

We are to support God's people in practical ways. Following is a prophetic Word, spoken by Jesus, regarding the Day of Judgment.

Matthew 25:35-40

³⁵ For I was hungry, and you gave Me *something* to eat; I was thirsty, and you gave Me *something* to drink; I was a stranger, and you invited Me in; ³⁶ naked, and you clothed Me; I was sick, and you visited Me; I was in prison, and you came to Me.' ³⁷ Then the righteous will answer Him, 'Lord, when did we see You hungry, and feed You, or thirsty, and give You *something* to drink? ³⁸ And when did we see You a stranger, and invite You in, or naked, and clothe You? ³⁹ When did we see You sick, or in prison, and come to You?' ⁴⁰ The King will answer and say to them, 'Truly I say to you, to the extent that you did it to one of these brothers of Mine, *even* the least *of them*, you did it to Me.'

The way we treat each other will not go unnoticed.

The Bible says we are to love our enemies. This is perfect love.

Matthew 5:43-48

⁴³ "You have heard that it was said, 'YOU SHALL LOVE YOUR NEIGHBOR and hate your enemy.' ⁴⁴ But I say to you, love your enemies and pray for those who persecute you, ⁴⁵ so that you may be sons of your Father who is in heaven; for He causes His sun to rise on *the* evil and *the* good, and sends rain on *the* righteous and *the* unrighteous. ⁴⁶ For if you love those who love you, what reward do you have? Do not even the tax collectors do the same? ⁴⁷ If you greet only your brothers, what more are you doing *than others*? Do not even the Gentiles do the same? ⁴⁸ Therefore you are to be perfect, as your heavenly Father is perfect.

I love this passage because it reminds me of my Father's perfect love. If it weren't for His perfect love, I'd still be lost in sin. Let your light shine upon the unloving.

Just like Ezra's twelve chosen men, we are also to support the Lord's House. We will be held accountable for what we allow in it.

There are only two accounts of situations in which Jesus displayed His anger for all to see. Keep in mind as you read that neither case was on the Sabbath.

Following is the first account.

John 2:13-16

¹³ The Passover of the Jews was near, and Jesus went up to Jerusalem. ¹⁴ And He found in the temple those who were selling oxen and sheep and doves, and the money changers seated *at their tables*. ¹⁵ And He made a scourge of cords, and drove *them* all out of the temple, with the sheep and the oxen; and He poured out the coins of the money changers and overturned their tables; ¹⁶ and to those who were selling the doves He said, "Take these things away; stop making My Father's house a place of business."

They were selling oxen, sheep and doves to be sacrificed. The people were to bring their sacrifices to the temple. They were not to buy them there. Jesus was angry because they made His Father's house a place of business. He was furious, but he was not out of control. He did not overturn the doves. He told those who were selling the doves to take them away. This is a perfect picture of righteous anger.

Here is the second account.

Mark 11:15, 16

¹⁵ Then they came to Jerusalem. And He entered the temple and began to drive out those who were buying and selling in the temple,

and overturned the tables of the money changers and the seats of those who were selling doves;

¹⁶ and He would not permit anyone to carry merchandise through the temple.

Both accounts were before the Passover, not on Passover or the Sabbath. Jesus became furious because the temple leaders were using the temple for business. They did this not once, but twice. The Sabbath is not the time for business nor is the temple the place for business. Remember, He is never changing. What upset Him then upsets Him now. Don't be found guilty of building your own business on the Lord's foundation. The church is never to be looked at as a business.

Just as the priests and Levites were holy before the Lord, so are we. Our bodies are God's holy and chosen vessels. We need to understand this. We are not to use them to commit acts of immorality. Remember that we are not alone, nor will we ever be again. The Holy Spirit has taken up permanent residence in us.

I Corinthians 6:17-20

¹⁷ But the one who joins himself to the Lord is one spirit *with Him*. ¹⁸ Flee immorality. Every *other* sin that a man commits is outside the body, but the immoral man sins against his own body. ¹⁹ Or do you not know that your body is a temple of the Holy Spirit who is in you, whom you have from God, and that you are not your own? ²⁰ For you have been bought with a price: therefore glorify God in your body.

Do not be seduced by evil-doers. You are the Lord's holy vessel. You will be held accountable for how you use it. Sexual sin is a sin against the Holy Spirit. You put Him through everything you do. He, alone, is the One we are and will be held accountable to. Don't be deceived. Don't put stock into the opinions of people, especially people of little character. On the Day of Judgment, their opinions will not matter.

Sadly, we began to worship money, rather than the Lord. We are not to be lovers of money; silver and gold are not holy. The abundance of money is a test, which most people fail. It easily causes us to fall into the sin of self-indulgence. The things we buy tend to cloud our view of, and take our focus from, the Lord. All we see is ourselves and our own little world. It may seem vast now, but in comparison to the world that God designed us for, it is small and meaningless.

We are to glorify the Lord with all we have. We will be held accountable for the finances given to us. What are you doing with your money? Are you giving the Lord His tithe, His ten percent? Are you taking care of your spouse, your children, your parents? Are you feeding the poor? Make sure you have your priorities in order. The Lord will take care of you. Put others first, then you'll never fall into self-indulgence.

Luke 16:12-14

12 And if you have not been faithful in the use of that which is another's, who will give you that which is your own? 13 No servant can serve two masters; for either he will hate the one and love the other, or else he will be devoted to one and despise the other. You cannot serve God and wealth."

14 Now the Pharisees, who were lovers of money, were listening to all these things and were scoffing at Him.

The Pharisees were lovers of money. This is a warning to all of us, but it was directed at religious leaders. This is an easy trap to fall in. King Solomon fell into this trap. He realized it and wrote the book of Ecclesiastes and spoke so clearly on vanity of vanities. He wrote that there is nothing new under the sun. Self-indulgence isn't all that it appears to be. It is deceptive. Self-indulgent people can never be satisfied. That is the curse that comes with self-indulgence.

Be faithful to the Lord with all that He has blessed you with and He will continue to bless you.

Matthew 25:31-34

³¹ "But when the Son of Man comes in His glory, and all the angels with Him, then He will sit on His glorious throne. ³² All the nations will be gathered before Him; and He will separate them from one another, as the shepherd separates the sheep from the goats; ³³ and He will put the sheep on His right, and the goats on the left.

³⁴ "Then the King will say to those on His right, 'Come, you who are blessed of My Father, inherit the kingdom prepared for you from the foundation of the world.

One day, we will be brought before the Lord. He will weigh all that is remaining from that which He gave us, after it has been burned in fire. The only thing remaining will be the souls of those who gave their lives to Him. Our reward in heaven will be based upon how many lives we've touched for Jesus. This is our purpose in life, and there will be an accounting.

Revelation 22:11-13

¹¹ "Let the one who does wrong, still do wrong; and the one who is filthy, still be filthy; and let the one who is righteous, still practice righteousness; and the one who is holy, still keep himself holy."

¹² "Behold, I am coming quickly, and My reward is with Me, to render to every man according to what he has done. ¹³ "I am the Alpha and the Omega, the first and the last, the beginning and the end."

There will always be those who fall for deception. This is why it is so important to learn the Word of God. The Bible is where we learn what pleases Him. Live your life above reproach. Practice righteousness and keep yourself holy. Hold yourself accountable for your words and actions. Accountability is a must, if we want to be fully restored. He loves you.

Have I Done My Best for Jesus

I wonder, have I done my best for Jesus,
Who died upon the cruel tree?
To think of His great sacrifice at Calv'ry!
I know my Lord expects the best from me.

Refrain

How many are the lost that I have lifted?
How many are the chained I've helped to free?
I wonder, have I done my best for Jesus,
When He has done so much for me?

The hours that I have wasted are so many,
The hours I've spent for Christ so few;
Because of all my lack of love for Jesus.
I wonder if His heart is breaking too.

Refrain

I wonder, have I cared enough for others,
Or have I let them die alone?
I might have helped a wand'rer to the Savior,
The seed of precious Life I might have sown.

Refrain

No longer will I stay within the valley,
I'll climb to mountain heights above;
The world is dying now for want of someone
To tell them of the Savior's matchless love.

Refrain

Written by: Ensign Edwin Young

DAY 18

REST

Rest: to get rest by lying down;
to cease from action or motion;
to be free from anxiety or disturbance;
to sit or lie fixed or supported;
to remain confident.

So far this week, we have gained a better understanding of service, fasting and accountability. Now we'll look at rest.

What does it mean when we are told, "He will give you rest?" What does it mean to "rest in the Lord?" There will be times when the Lord tells us to rest. At the same time, everyone else will be saying we should be doing something. When this happens, put your trust in the Lord and rest. We need to learn how to rest, to stop what we are doing, and wait on the Lord. Resting is a choice. It is a decision that we have to make in order to get a new perspective on the situation we find ourselves in. This is a time when we completely fix our attention on the Lord and connect ourselves to Him, choosing to separate ourselves from all other influences and letting go of our own ideas and plans. This is where we come to be strengthened and enlightened by the Holy Spirit.

Remember, He knows the past, present and future. There is

no better place to go in order to gain understanding. "Resting in the Lord" is giving Him your concerns. When you do this, "He will give you rest." Peace will come and anxiety will leave. You will have the assurance that He is with you and will support you and your decision, regardless of how difficult it appears. Then you will have the confidence you need to carry on, because you will know that He is with you.

Let's take another look at Ezra and those with him when they camped at the river of Ahava.

Ezra 8:15, 21

15 Now I assembled them at the river that runs to Ahava, where we camped for three days; and when I observed the people and the priests, I did not find any Levites there.

21 Then I proclaimed a fast there at the river of Ahava, that we might humble ourselves before our God to seek from Him a safe journey for us, our little ones, and all our possessions.

Ezra and those with him began this journey with a three-day rest. They fasted and prayed at the river for three days. This is what resting in the arms of the Lord looks like. They were seeking His face and favor. This was an intense time. They were aware of the letters which were written to the kings by their enemies. They knew they were entering enemy territory and were not about to rush into it. They were first going to take time to rest in the Lord. They needed to know beyond a shadow of doubt that He was with them and was going to be with them on this long and potentially dangerous journey. They needed His protection.

Ezra and those with him knew they were called by the Lord for this purpose. However, they also knew they were not capable of defending themselves from attack or ambush. They understood that they were capable of doing only so much, and they needed the Lord to do the rest. They needed His protection. The Lord was faithful to them and poured out His peace upon them.

Three days was also enough time for everyone to stop and realize the challenges ahead and the great responsibility that was entrusted to them. This was a time of humility, so they humbly sought the Lord's protection. This was a time of unity. The Lord loved every second of it. He would surely protect and bless His people along the way.

They had been in captivity for over seventy years. Their journey lasted five months (Ez. 7:9). Envision the joy that filled their hearts when they first saw Jerusalem and the temple. The relief and joy they felt must have been overwhelming; relief, because the Lord had fulfilled His promises to keep them safe; joy, because they were finally home. I am sure this was a time of reuniting with family and friends who had gone on before them. What a wonderful time it must have been!

Ezra also ended this journey with a three-day rest.

Ezra 8:32, 33a

³² Thus we came to Jerusalem and remained there three days.

³³ On the fourth day the silver and the gold and the utensils were weighed out…

They waited three days before performing any of their duties.

Ezra, who "had set his heart to study the law of the Lord and to practice it and to teach His statutes and ordinances in Israel," knew how to rest and take time alone with the Lord. He was in Israel for a specific purpose and we know by now that he took this responsibility very seriously. Ezra needed to know to whom they were to weigh out the silver, gold and utensils. He was not going to hand them over to anyone without clear direction from the Lord. I can picture Ezra walking around Jerusalem, praying for its peace and future. Then on the fourth day, the silver, gold and utensils were weighed in the temple, into the hand of Meremoth with the others observing.

This makes me think of when we finally get to heaven. We'll have a few days to take it all in before we do anything. It will be a time of thanksgiving and celebration.

Let me share a time with you, when I had to lay my desires and plans down and seek the Lord's face. I needed to know His plan. I needed peace, and it could only have come from Him. When my son was eighteen years old, he came to inform me of his plans to join the Army. I was furious. I felt like the enemy was trying to take my son from me. I felt betrayed and could not stop crying. During this time, we were at war. I was fearful that my son would be killed or emotionally messed up. I had witnessed first-hand these things happening to our veterans in the Vietnam War, so had reason to be afraid.

Then I realized I needed to seek the Lord's face and gain His understanding, so I began to fast and pray. My tears continued to flow down my cheeks with every prayer of absolute despair. I was desperate for the Lord's peace. Three days later, the Lord clearly told me my son would be okay in the Army, and that he would come out not only a man, but a man of God. Immediately, the peace of the Lord fell on me and remained on me, throughout my son's military years. I cannot imagine the fear I would have had to endure during those years, if I hadn't taken the time to rest in the Lord and seek His understanding. The Lord was faithful. He gave me a promise to stand on. He answered my prayers, certainly not in the way I thought He would, but in His own perfect way.

We all need to make it a habit never to make a long-term commitment without resting in the Lord first. Take time to pray about the situation, regardless of how good or godly it appears to be. This three-day rest will always follow with peace and a clear understanding of what God's desire is. When something is from the Lord, He will give you time to honor Him by bringing it to Him before you make a commitment. Knowing this, we can assume that if someone demands an immediate answer, he or she is not from the Lord. Do yourself a favor and just say no. Inevitably, you will find that your answer was the right one, if for only one reason: you refused to say yes without hearing from the Lord. By taking the time to rest and seek His direction, we make sure we are not stepping out on our own strength or ability. This is where we prove ourselves to be loyal to Him and His plan and His purpose, not our own.

Romans 8:28

²⁸ And we know that God causes all things to work together for good to those who love God, to those who are called according to *His* purpose.

Rest patiently and be content in knowing everything is working together for good. After accepting Christ as our Savior, we go into a time of preparation. We know He is preparing us for something, we just don't know exactly what it is. So we commit ourselves to learning His Word and growing in our walk with Him. We rest patiently in His arms, knowing He is moving in our midst. He will first open doors for us that seem menial. However, nothing is menial to the Lord.

Let's see through His Word what this looks like.

Exodus 3:1-2, 7, 10

¹ Now Moses was pasturing the flock of Jethro his father-in-law, the priest of Midian; and he led the flock to the west side of the wilderness and came to Horeb, the mountain of God. ² The angel of the LORD appeared to him in a blazing fire from the midst of a

bush; and he looked, and behold, the bush was burning with fire, yet the bush was not consumed.

⁷ The LORD said, "I have surely seen the affliction of My people who are in Egypt, and have given heed to their cry because of their taskmasters, for I am aware of their sufferings.

¹⁰ Therefore, come now, and I will send you to Pharaoh, so that you may bring My people, the sons of Israel, out of Egypt."

Moses had been waiting on the Lord for forty years in Midian. He got married, became a shepherd and was mentored by his father-in-law, Jethro, the priest of Midian. Shepherding sheep was considered a menial task. However, Moses would soon become the shepherd of God's people. Forty years doesn't seem soon. However, when Moses was called by the Lord to go back to Egypt and deliver His people from Pharaoh, it felt like way too soon. Moses needed those forty years to prepare himself for the next forty. They would be forty years of intense ministry, with people who were just as stubborn as his sheep were. Moses had to prove himself accountable for his own flock before being given God's.

Jesus was tested in the desert for forty days. This was also a time of resting in the arms of the Lord. Jesus stood on the Word of God during His testing. Notice that Jesus' time of testing and waiting was forty days rather than forty years.

During times of testing, we need to lean on the Lord and let Him be our support. If we don't have the Word of God in us, we will have nothing to stand on. It is our firm foundation. We would be wise to realize that we don't have to stay out in the desert for forty years walking around the same mountain. We can cross over it and be on our way. The sooner we overcome the obstacles in our life, the sooner our testing will end.

We have seen what resting in the Lord looks like. Now we'll

see how He provided a time of rest for us.

Genesis 2:1-3

¹ Thus the heavens and the earth were completed, and all their hosts. ² By the seventh day God completed His work which He had done, and He rested on the seventh day from all His work which He had done. ³ Then God blessed the seventh day and sanctified it, because in it He rested from all His work which God had created and made.

We see here that God created the heavens and earth in six days and rested on the seventh. What this passage says next is of utmost importance. "Then God blessed the seventh day and sanctified it." This is the first holy day mentioned in the Bible. God set it apart to be a day of blessing and rest. These two go hand-in-hand. We cannot expect to be blessed if we are not willing to rest.

The Sabbath rest is the fourth of the Ten Commandments, the only one that comes with instructions. The first four Commandments regard our walk with the Lord. The last six are in regard to how we treat others. Since this book is on our restoration as the temple of God, it is of utmost importance that we clearly understand the first four commandments before we move on to the next six.

Exodus 20:1, 8-12

¹ Then God spoke all these words, saying,

⁸ "Remember the sabbath day, to keep it holy. ⁹ Six days you shall labor and do all your work, ¹⁰ but the seventh day is a sabbath of the LORD your God; *in it* you shall not do any work, you or your son or your daughter, your male or your female servant or your cattle or your sojourner who stays with you. ¹¹ For in six days the LORD made the heavens and the earth, the sea and all that is in them, and rested on the seventh day; therefore the LORD

blessed the sabbath day and made it holy.

¹² "Six days you are to do your work, but on the seventh day you shall cease from labor so that your ox and your donkey may rest, and the son of your female slave, as well as your stranger, may refresh themselves.

We are to "Remember the sabbath day, to keep it holy." Notice it's not the Sabbath hour. He then tells us how to keep it holy. Three times, He says we are to do all of our work in six days. Why? Because on "the seventh day... you shall not do any work." Why? Then every person and animal with us can rest and be refreshed. Why? Because it "is a sabbath of the Lord your God" and "the Lord blessed the Sabbath day and made it holy." It is His day. He blessed it. He made it holy. We need to treat it that way.

Unfortunately, the only Sabbath days most Christians fully respect are Christmas and Easter. It is truly heart-breaking how far from here the church has strayed. We need to get back to the basics. We have sold ourselves short by allowing the Sabbath to become just another day. Every Sabbath day should be spent with family and friends as though it were Christmas or Easter. We are to honor and praise the Lord in it, keeping it holy, for it is His day. Twice the Lord said we are not to allow the sojourner or stranger with us to work. He said this so we don't put it into our heads that it is okay to go out and have unbelievers serve us on the Sabbath. It is not okay. They, too, need a time to rest and be refreshed.

When I first came back to the Lord and was reading the Ten Commandments, He laid the Sabbath rest heavy on my heart. He brought me back to my childhood to see the contrast between the Sabbath then and now. Back then, most businesses were closed. It was a family day. The neighborhood for the most part was quiet and free of all work. The Lord then told me He wanted me to honor the

Sabbath rest, as many had done during my childhood. So I obeyed Him.

It became the happiest day for my kids and me. We all looked forward to a day of rest. We would often go to the beach or stay home and have a barbecue. We knew that most Christians were going out. In fact, most of them thought I was being legalistic. Unfortunately, about seven years later, I gave in and allowed my kids, who were in high school at the time, to go out with their friends from church. Then I started going out. I can tell you now, by looking back, it was a big mistake. I should not have allowed this to happen. It began to tear at the fiber of our family. The Sabbath had been the only day we really spent time together and encouraged each other. We gave this up for acquaintances. My kids needed my advice and guidance more than ever. Instead, however, they were getting it from those who didn't take their walk with the Lord as seriously as we had. This was not honoring God. It was disobedience. It was sin.

The Sabbath rest was given as a commandment for our good. God blessed the day and we are to keep it holy.

Let's take a look at Jesus on the Sabbath.

Mark 6:2

² When the Sabbath came, He began to teach in the synagogue; and the many listeners were astonished, saying, "Where did this man *get* these things, and what is *this* wisdom given to Him, and such miracles as these performed by His hands?

Luke 4:16

¹⁶ And He came to Nazareth, where He had been brought up; and as was His custom, He entered the synagogue on the Sabbath, and stood up to read.

Luke 4:31

³¹ And He came down to Capernaum, a city of Galilee, and He was teaching them on the Sabbath;

Jesus taught and read in the synagogue on the Sabbath, no matter where He was. It didn't matter which synagogue He went to. What mattered was that He observed the Sabbath rest by honoring His Father on it.

Churches are different. However, as long as the Word of God is being taught and the Lord is being exalted, it is good. We can learn different things at different churches, because pastors have different insights into the Word of God. We should be open to hear and receive all that the Lord has for us. I doubt very seriously if you can learn it all from one person. We should be open to hear what the Lord is saying to and through other pastors. This is how we gain balance in our walk.

Luke 6:6-16

⁶ On another Sabbath He entered the synagogue and was teaching; and there was a man there whose right hand was withered. ⁷ The scribes and the Pharisees were watching Him closely to see if He healed on the Sabbath, so that they might find *reason* to accuse Him. ⁸ But He knew what they were thinking, and He said to the man with the withered hand, "Get up and come forward!" And he got up and came forward. ⁹ And Jesus said to them, "I ask you, is it lawful to do good or to do harm on the Sabbath, to save a life or to destroy it?" ¹⁰ After looking around at them all, He said to him, "Stretch out your hand!" And he did so; and his hand was restored. ¹¹ But they themselves were filled with rage, and discussed together what they might do to Jesus.

¹² It was at this time that He went off to the mountain to pray, and He spent the whole night in prayer to God. ¹³ And when day

came, He called His disciples to Him and chose twelve of them, whom He also named as apostles: **¹⁴ Simon, whom He also named Peter, and Andrew his brother; and James and John; and Philip and Bartholomew; ¹⁵ and Matthew and Thomas; James *the son* of Alphaeus, and Simon who was called the Zealot; ¹⁶ Judas *the son* of James, and Judas Iscariot, who became a traitor.**

Jesus healed the man with the withered hand in the synagogue, on the Sabbath. This disturbed the Pharisees because they were so legalistic that they looked at healing as work. Jesus looked at it from a different point of view. He saw it as doing good.

After Jesus healed the man, He went off to the mountain where He spent the night in prayer with His Father. No doubt He was seeking direction regarding those who were to be His disciples. In the morning, He chose twelve and also named them as apostles. This is a great picture of Jesus resting in the Father's arms.

God blessed the Sabbath and made it holy. Jesus said it is a day to do good and save lives. It is a day to hear from the Father through His Word, and to see His manifested power working for the good in our lives. On the Sabbath, we should see Jesus not only as Teacher, but also as Healer and Savior as well.

Obey the Sabbath rest. Request the day off, if possible. If you are not able to take it off, then make one of your days off a day of rest. That is what matters. Obey the rest of the command by not allowing others to serve you. Remember that God is a God of order. We are wise to order our steps and make provisions for the Sabbath rest. Get into the habit of getting gas and groceries during your six days of work. Buying food for a picnic lunch, while travelling on the Sabbath, is a great alternative to eating out. You can start your Sabbath rest in the morning or during the prior evening. There are lots of places to attend evening services on both days. This is great for those who have to work or are traveling. You can almost always find a service that will fit into any schedule. If you choose to start in the evening, then you can eat out the following night.

I mentioned before that we cannot lead others to Christ if we are dogmatic and unbending in our beliefs. We serve a God of grace. What matters to Him is that we make an effort to keep His day holy. He knows your heart. Be at peace, enjoy the day and trust that He is in it.

By honoring the Sabbath rest, you will get more done in six days than you ever did in seven. There will be an increased desire among those in your family to go to church and honor the Lord. It will give you time to see how the Lord's hand has been on you throughout the week. You will become more grateful for what you have. You and your children will even feel safer, knowing that you honor the Lord. You will know He is with you. There will be unity in your family like never before. You will gain confidence in the Lord, and with that comes incredible peace.

Rest in the Lord and enter His rest by obeying and keeping the Sabbath holy.

More About Jesus

More about Jesus would I know,
More of His grace to others show;
More of His saving fullness see,
More of His love Who died for me.

Refrain

More, more about Jesus,
More, more about Jesus;
More of His saving fullness see,
More of His love Who died for me.

More about Jesus let me learn,
More of His holy will discern;
Spirit of God, my teacher be,
Showing the things of Christ to me.

Refrain

More about Jesus; in His Word,
Holding communion with my Lord;
Hearing His voice in every line,
Making each faithful saying mine.

Refrain

More about Jesus; on His throne,
Riches in glory all His own;
More of His kingdom's sure increase;
More of His coming, Prince of Peace.

Refrain

Written by: Eliza E. Hewitt

DAY 19
SIN

Sin: an offense against religious or moral law;
a vitiated state of human nature in which
the self is estranged from God.
Offense: a cause or occasion of sin: stumbling block;
Stumbling block: an obstacle to progress.

Sin separates us from God and is always an obstacle to progress. What is sin for one person may not be sin for another person.

Let's see how things are going in Jerusalem. Remember Ezra and those with him have prayerfully delivered the gold, silver and utensils to the priests, offered burnt offering to the Lord and delivered the kings' edicts to the king's satraps and governors in the provinces beyond the River. They are now supporting the people and the house of God.

Ezra was still to appoint magistrates and judges to judge all the people in the provinces beyond the River. He was also to teach the law to those ignorant of them. Their laws, along with the laws of the king, would be the laws everyone, including their enemies, would have to live by.

Finally, the law of God would be restored in Israel. Once

the law was upheld, order and blessings in abundance would surely follow. In Ezra's sight, this was certainly an exciting time for the nation of Israel. He was doing everything correctly and responsibly. Now, let's see how seriously the others in Jerusalem were taking their responsibilities.

Ezra 9:1-4

¹ Now when these things had been completed, the princes approached me, saying, "The people of Israel and the priests and the Levites have not separated themselves from the peoples of the lands, according to their abominations, *those* of the Canaanites, the Hittites, the Perizzites, the Jebusites, the Ammonites, the Moabites, the Egyptians and the Amorites. ² For they have taken some of their daughters as *wives* for themselves and for their sons, so that the holy race has intermingled with the peoples of the lands; indeed, the hands of the princes and the rulers have been foremost in this unfaithfulness." ³ When I heard about this matter, I tore my garment and my robe, and pulled some of the hair from my head and my beard, and sat down appalled. ⁴ Then everyone who trembled at the words of the God of Israel on account of the unfaithfulness of the exiles gathered to me, and I sat appalled until the evening offering.

Ezra is appalled. He has just been told that the people of Israel, the priests and the Levites had been marrying the people of the land. This meant they had defiled the holy race. They were not obeying the Jewish law. How could Ezra impose the law on those outside the camp, when those inside the camp weren't living according to it? He realizes his job is way bigger than he anticipated. Being a man of God who reveres the Lord, he is heart-broken. His heart is breaking for the Lord. However, he realizes this is not a surprise to the Lord; He has seen it all.

They were a holy race. They were not to intermarry. They were to keep themselves holy. God knew that if they intermarried, they would be carried away by false gods of their wives.

Deuteronomy : 14:2

² "For you are a holy people to the LORD your God, and the LORD has chosen you to be a people for His own possession out of all the peoples who are on the face of the earth.

They are God's holy and chosen people. They were to be a people for His own possession. He called them out from all the peoples of the world. They were the race from which the Messiah would come.

There isn't anything anyone can do to change that. They are and will always be under His protection. He has held them responsible for their sin by scattering them throughout the world for it. However, for the last sixty years, He has been restoring and gathering them back to their homeland, just as He promised. He is leading them and He will protect them. Their enemies are great in number, but no match for God.

There are laws specifically for Jews. It is sin for them not to obey them. These laws set Israel apart from the rest of the world. These laws are mainly about circumcision and foods they can and cannot eat. They were not meant for the rest of us. We are not under the law. We are saved by grace.

Just as Ezra knew that God had seen the sin of the people, you can be sure that your sin is not committed in secret, either. Following is scripture about what King David did to cover his secret sin and how God reacted to it. It is the Word of God spoken to David through Nathan the prophet.

II Samuel 12:9-14

⁹ Why have you despised the word of the LORD by doing evil in His sight? You have struck down Uriah the Hittite with the sword, have taken his wife to be your wife, and have killed him with the sword of the sons of Ammon. ¹⁰ Now therefore, the sword shall never depart from your house, because you have despised Me and have taken the wife of Uriah the Hittite to be your wife.' ¹¹ Thus says the LORD, 'Behold, I will raise up evil against you from your own household; I will even take your wives before your eyes and give *them* **to your companion, and he will lie with your wives in broad daylight. ¹² Indeed you did it secretly, but I will do this thing before all Israel, and under the sun.'" ¹³ Then David said to Nathan, "I have sinned against the LORD." And Nathan said to David, "The LORD also has taken away your sin; you shall not die. ¹⁴ However, because by this deed you have given occasion to the enemies of the LORD to blaspheme, the child also that is born to you shall surely die."**

David committed adultery and murder. He broke the law of God. He paid for this sin for the rest of his life, even though God forgave him. There was a price to be paid for Uriah's death. It was the child Bathsheba was carrying and more. This prophecy was fulfilled. Absalom, David's son, took David's wives for himself, in broad daylight, before all of Israel. The price that was paid for their sin didn't go unnoticed by the people of Israel.

King David wrote this after being confronted by Nathan the prophet.

Psalm 51:4

⁴ Against You, You only, I have sinned
**   And done what is evil in Your sight,**
**   So that You are justified when You speak**

And blameless when You judge

When we sin, it is against God and God alone. It may hurt others, but it is against His command, not theirs. It doesn't matter what the others involved think or how they feel about the sin. It is still sin. David's sin with Bathsheba was sin, regardless of her willingness to participate in it.

We are always being watched by God and those around us. We are being used as examples for both the good and the bad we do.

Today, those who commit adultery pay for it as well. And not only they, but their entire household will pay: "Behold, I will raise up evil against you from your own household." Today, we see and hear the anger and evil that comes from some of the children in broken homes. Their anger seems to have no end. We also see in violent neighborhoods the curse that murder brings with it: "The sword shall never depart from your house." However, the good news is we can break this curse with the blood of Jesus.

What if a person sins unknowingly? What does the Bible say about that?

Leviticus 5:17-19

17 "Now if a person sins and does any of the things which the LORD has commanded not to be done, though he was unaware, still he is guilty and shall bear his punishment. 18 He is then to bring to the priest a ram without defect from the flock, according to your valuation, for a guilt offering. So the priest shall make atonement for him concerning his error in which he sinned unintentionally and did not know *it*, and it will be forgiven him. 19 It is a guilt offering; he was certainly guilty before the LORD."

Ignorance of sin does not make us innocent from sin. The blood of a ram without defect would atone for it. There isn't anything that will change this. It is a spiritual law. Before the Lord we are certainly guilty, not possibly guilty.

However, the prophet Isaiah spoke of One to come who would be the final guilt offering. Let's read what he had to say about Him.

Isaiah 53:10-12

¹⁰ But the LORD was pleased
>   **To crush Him, putting Him to grief;**
>   **If He would render Himself as a guilt offering,**
>   **He will see His offspring,**
>   **He will prolong His days,**
>   **And the good pleasure of the LORD will prosper in His hand.**

¹¹ As a result of the anguish of His soul,
>   **He will see it and be satisfied;**
>   **By His knowledge the Righteous One,**
>   **My Servant, will justify the many,**
>   **As He will bear their iniquities.**

¹² Therefore, I will allot Him a portion with the great,
>   **And He will divide the booty with the strong;**
>   **Because He poured out Himself to death,**
>   **And was numbered with the transgressors;**
>   **Yet He Himself bore the sin of many,**
>   **And interceded for the transgressors.**

Jesus is the guilt offering. He died on the cross for our sins before we were even born. When we claim Him for ourselves and His blood atones for our sin, past, present and future, and removes the curse of eternal death. His blood will never lose its power. Then, on the Day of Judgment when the Father looks at us, He will see the blood of Jesus instead of our sin.

Does this mean we can continue in our sin? No. We would all be wise to read the books of law in the Old Testament. We know that God is the same yesterday, today and tomorrow. What honored Him then, honors Him now. What He considered evil then, He considers evil now. Let's see what Jesus said about the Law and those who do not uphold it

Matthew 5:17-19

¹⁷ "Do not think that I came to abolish the Law or the Prophets; I did not come to abolish but to fulfill. ¹⁸ For truly I say to you, until heaven and earth pass away, not the smallest letter or stroke shall pass from the Law until all is accomplished. ¹⁹ Whoever then annuls one of the least of these commandments, and teaches others *to do* the same, shall be called least in the kingdom of heaven; but whoever keeps and teaches *them*, he shall be called great in the kingdom of heaven.

Jesus did not come to abolish the Law or the Prophets. The Law will remain until heaven and earth pass away. We are not to annul one of the least of these commandments or teach others to do so. Through the indwelling Holy Spirit, we are quickened to do what is right. He will speak to our spirit when we are doing something wrong. He is the One who helps us to uphold the Law.

Jesus did not want us to be weighed down with the Law. Therefore, He made it simple.

Matthew 22:.36-40

³⁶ "Teacher, which is the great commandment in the Law?" ³⁷ And He said to him, " 'YOU SHALL LOVE THE LORD YOUR GOD WITH ALL YOUR HEART, AND WITH ALL YOUR SOUL, AND WITH ALL YOUR MIND.' ³⁸ This is the great and foremost commandment. ³⁹ The second is like it, 'YOU SHALL LOVE YOUR NEIGHBOR AS YOURSELF.' ⁴⁰ On these two

commandments depend the whole Law and the Prophets."

Love God and people. Treat people the way you want to be treated.

When we've allowed something to come between us and God, He will ask us to remove it. If we don't, it is sin. It is disobedience. It will separate us from God. Let's look at a conversation between Jesus and a rich young man to better understand this.

Matthew 19:16-26

16 **And someone came to Him and said, "Teacher, what good thing shall I do that I may obtain eternal life?"** **17** **And He said to him, "Why are you asking Me about what is good? There is *only* One who is good; but if you wish to enter into life, keep the commandments."** **18** **Then he *said to Him, "Which ones?" And Jesus said, "YOU SHALL NOT COMMIT MURDER; YOU SHALL NOT COMMIT ADULTERY; YOU SHALL NOT STEAL; YOU SHALL NOT BEAR FALSE WITNESS;** **19** **HONOR YOUR FATHER AND MOTHER; and YOU SHALL LOVE YOUR NEIGHBOR AS YOURSELF."** **20** **The young man *said to Him, "All these things I have kept; what am I still lacking?"** **21** **Jesus said to him, "If you wish to be complete, go *and* sell your possessions and give to *the* poor, and you will have treasure in heaven; and come, follow Me."** **22** **But when the young man heard this statement, he went away grieving; for he was one who owned much property.**

23 **And Jesus said to His disciples, "Truly I say to you, it is hard for a rich man to enter the kingdom of heaven.** **24** **Again I say to you, it is easier for a camel to go through the eye of a needle, than for a rich man to enter the kingdom of God."** **25** **When the disciples heard *this*, they were very astonished and said, "Then who can be saved?"** **26** **And looking at them Jesus said to them, "With people this is impossible, but with God all things are possible."**

Jesus says that to have eternal life, we must keep the commandments and follow Him. This is not about being poor in order to follow Jesus. It is about putting our faith in God and not in our wealth. Surely the Lord would have returned the rich man's wealth to him. The problem was that this man worshipped his money. Jesus knew that the moment He laid eyes on him. This is a warning for all of us. We are not to make an idol out of our money.

Jesus is love, and all that he did directs us to be the same.

John 13:34-35

³⁴ A new commandment I give to you, that you love one another, even as I have loved you, that you also love one another. ³⁵ By this all men will know that you are My disciples, if you have love for one another."

Our walk with Him is all about loving God and loving people. Not doing this is sin. In fact, it is the basis of all sin. How much easier could it possibly be? Living a sin-free life should not be a burden. It should be an absolute joy for us and all of those He brings on our path.

John 8:34

³⁴ Jesus answered them, "Truly, truly, I say to you, everyone who commits sin is the slave of sin.

He came to set us free. Don't allow sin to keep you in bondage.

John 8:32-24

²³ And He was saying to them, "You are from below, I am from above; you are of this world, I am not of this world. ²⁴ Therefore I said to you that you will die in your sins; for unless you believe that I am *He*, you will die in your sins."

In Egypt, when the angel of death saw the blood on the door

posts and mantles of the Israelites, it passed over their home and didn't take the life of their firstborn. In this same way, Jesus' blood that was spilt on the cross will protect us from death. The blood from His hands nailed to the cross, represents the blood on the door posts, and the blood on His forehead from the crown of thorns, represents the blood on the mantle. He is the door. All who enter in will be saved.

John 10:7-11

⁷ So Jesus said to them again, "Truly, truly, I say to you, I am the door of the sheep. ⁸ All who came before Me are thieves and robbers, but the sheep did not hear them. ⁹ I am the door; if anyone enters through Me, he will be saved, and will go in and out and find pasture. ¹⁰ The thief comes only to steal and kill and destroy; I came that they may have life, and have *it* abundantly.

¹¹ "I am the good shepherd; the good shepherd lays down His life for the sheep.

He chose to die for your sin. Enter into His Presence and be saved. He is the door to eternal life.

Saved By the Blood

We're saved by the blood
That was drawn from the side
Of Jesus our Lord,
When He languished and died.

Refrain

Hallelujah to God,
For redemption so free;
Hallelujah, hallelujah,
Dear Savior, to Thee.

O yes, 'tis the blood
Of the Lamb that was slain;
He conquered the grave,
And He liveth again.

Refrain

We're saved by the blood;
We are sealed by its power;
'Tis life to the soul,
And is hope every hour.

Refrain

That blood is a fount
Where the vilest may go
And wash till their souls
Shall be whiter than snow.

Refrain

We're saved by the blood,
Hallelujah again;
We're saved by the blood,
Hallelujah, Amen.

Refrain

Written by: S.J. Henderson

DAY  20
CONFESSION

Confession: an act of confessing; especially:
a disclosure of one's sin
in the sacrament of reconciliation;
a written or oral acknowledgment of guilt
by a party accused of an offense.
Confess: to tell or make known;
to disclose one's faults; admit.
Admit: to concede as true or valid.

So far this week, we've gained understanding regarding service, fasting, accountability, rest and sin. Today, we will see how confession works. Confession is the key to forgiveness. God cannot forgive us until we ask Him to. Jesus said, "You have not because you ask not." By asking for forgiveness, we are acknowledging our guilt and sin. We are putting our sin under the blood of the Lamb. Then we are reconciled.

Yesterday, we left Ezra sitting in the street, appalled due to the blatant sin of Israel. He was disgusted with the lack of reverence they had shown to God. The following questions must have been going through his mind. Have they forgotten where they just came from? Have they forgotten the cause of our captivity? How could they be turning away from God and His laws already? Ezra felt defeated before he ever started implementing the new laws of the land. Let's see how he's doing today. Try to feel his broken heart as you read his prayer.

Ezra 9:5-15

5 But at the evening offering I arose from my humiliation, even with my garment and my robe torn, and I fell on my knees and stretched out my hands to the LORD my God; 6 and I said, "O my God, I am ashamed and embarrassed to lift up my face to You, my God, for our iniquities have risen above our heads and our guilt has grown even to the heavens. 7 Since the days of our fathers to this day we *have been* in great guilt, and on account of our iniquities we, our kings *and* our priests have been given into the hand of the kings of the lands, to the sword, to captivity and to plunder and to open shame, as *it is* this day. 8 But now for a brief moment grace has been *shown* from the LORD our God, to leave us an escaped remnant and to give us a peg in His holy place, that our God may enlighten our eyes and grant us a little reviving in our bondage. 9 For we are slaves; yet in our bondage our God has not forsaken us, but has extended lovingkindness to us in the sight of the kings of Persia, to give us reviving to raise up the house of our God, to restore its ruins and to give us a wall in Judah and Jerusalem.

10 "Now, our God, what shall we say after this? For we have forsaken Your commandments, 11 which You have commanded by Your servants the prophets, saying, 'The land which you are entering to possess is an unclean land with the uncleanness of the peoples of the lands, with their abominations which have filled it from end to end *and* with their impurity. 12 So now do not give your daughters to their sons nor take their daughters to your sons, and never seek their peace or their prosperity, that you may be strong and eat the good *things* of the land and leave *it* as an inheritance to your sons

forever.' ¹³ After all that has come upon us for our evil deeds and our great guilt, since You our God have requited *us* less than our iniquities *deserve*, and have given us an escaped remnant as this, ¹⁴ shall we again break Your commandments and intermarry with the peoples who commit these abominations? Would You not be angry with us to the point of destruction, until there is no remnant nor any who escape? ¹⁵ O LORD God of Israel, You are righteous, for we have been left an escaped remnant, *as it is* this day; behold, we are before You in our guilt, for no one can stand before You because of this."

Ezra is in front of the house of God. He is openly confessing their sin to God. He is on his knees with his hands stretched out in a manner of submission. He is ashamed and embarrassed even to look at God, due to their sin. He acknowledges the fact that their sin has reached heaven and is of no surprise to God. He then states two facts: First, it is because of sin they are currently in the hands of their enemies and have openly been put to shame. Second, this is not the first time they've broken the commandments and intermarried with the peoples who commit abominations. These people worshipped false gods. After this confession, he reminds Israel that they are still slaves to Persia. Only by God's grace and loving kindness were they given a little reviving. Because of God, the kings of Persia allowed them to rebuild the temple. He asks God, "What shall we say after this?" In other words, there is nothing that can be said to make this right. He clearly states the sin according to how it is written in the Word of God. He is letting God and the people of Israel know why he is appalled. He also acknowledges that only by God's mercy will they escape destruction. Ezra calls God righteous, and then humbly submits himself and the people to Him for judgment.

Ezra 10:1

¹ Now while Ezra was praying and making confession, weeping and

prostrating himself before the house of God, a very large assembly, men, women and children, gathered to him from Israel; for the people wept bitterly.

Ezra was not guilty of these things. However, being a priest and sent by the king, he was in a position of authority over the people of Israel. Therefore, he took responsibility for their sin. While Ezra was confessing, the people were weeping bitterly. They were being convicted of their sin and reminded of the fact that God, according to His Word, could destroy them because of it. Ezra was wise to confess. He knew that only by God's mercy would they be saved from destruction.

We can learn by Ezra's example how to win God's people back to Him. We would be wise, as Ezra was, to get down on our knees and pray for God's forgiveness for the sin that surrounds us. We can begin with the sins of greed, immorality, rebelliousness and murder, to name a few. This is known today as identification repentance, which is a type of prayer that identifies with and confesses before God, the corporate sins of one's nation, people, church or family.

It is amazing to see how lives can be changed through the prayers of other people. It is not necessary for those being prayed for to be there or even to be in agreement. Identification repentance removes strongholds by disempowering them. The stronghold of the sin is loosened through prayer, and then those once bound by that sin can free themselves from it once and for all.

II Chronicles 7:14

¹⁴ and My people who are called by My name humble themselves and pray and seek My face and turn from their wicked ways, then I will hear from heaven, will forgive their sin and will heal their land.

When we humble ourselves and pray and seek the Lord with

repentant hearts, He will hear us and forgive our sin and heal our land.

Let's see what the John the apostle said about confession.

1 John 1:9

⁹ If we confess our sins, He is faithful and righteous to forgive us our sins and to cleanse us from all unrighteousness.

Remember, the guilt offering is for sin we are not aware of. However, it is our responsibility to confess the sin in our lives that we are aware of. In doing so, we put it under the blood of the Lamb and are forgiven, cleansed from all unrighteousness. Because we are priests, we can go directly to the Lord and confess our sins. He is Faithful and Righteous to forgive us. We need to get into the habit of confessing as soon as we realize we've sinned. This helps us to stop sinning.

I knelt at the side of my bed every night for months confessing my sin of smoking cigarettes. I knew I was killing myself with cigarettes. However, smoking had a very strong hold on me. Cigarette smoking is not only bad for our bodies but, in my case, I am also allergic to tobacco. My doctor told me I would not live to be forty if I didn't quit smoking. When I finally got sick of hearing myself confess the same thing every night, I asked the Lord to completely remove the desire to smoke from me and to help me quit. Shortly after that prayer, the Lord spoke to my spirit and told me I was never to smoke again. I quit that day, and have not smoked since. Looking back, I realize I needed to come to the place of desperation and futility, before I was truly willing to give it up. I now realize I didn't have the power from within myself to do it. I needed the Lord's power. It was His spoken Word to me that day, which freed me from smoking. "We have not, because we ask not." He is our Deliverer.

Let's look at another type of confession. Following are Words Jesus spoke in the Sermon on the Mount.

Matthew 5:23-25

23 Therefore if you are presenting your offering at the altar, and there remember that your brother has something against you, 24 leave your offering there before the altar and go; first be reconciled to your brother, and then come and present your offering. 25 Make friends quickly with your opponent at law while you are with him on the way, so that your opponent may not hand you over to the judge, and the judge to the officer, and you be thrown into prison.

When we wrong someone, we need to humble ourselves and take responsibility for it. This is another aspect of confession which is very important. This is when others see that we not only talk the talk, but we also walk the walk. Though admitting one's wrongs is very embarrassing and humiliating, it is perhaps the fastest way to gain the respect of others. This needs to become part of our daily walk. We will stop wronging people, once we start taking responsibility for our actions.

If you have made a habit of wronging people, it will take time for them to take your apologies seriously. It takes time to prove to others that we have changed and we are not turning back. The more pain you've caused, the longer this process will take. However, what matters is your heart. That is what the Lord is looking at.

The Lord has not abandoned us to our sin. We are not alone. He sent the Holy Spirit, who will convict us of our sin. He also empowers us to overcome it, in His perfect timing. Remember, we are all a work in progress.

On the other hand, however, the devil will try to overwhelm and condemn us with our sin. Dismiss him and every word of condemnation he throws at you. Don't allow his guilt tactics to deceive or discourage you.

Romans 8:1

¹ Therefore there is now no condemnation for those who are in Christ Jesus.

We are under grace, which means the Lord will give us the time we need to overcome the sin that has held us captive. He is merciful. He sees our heart and knows we are trying.

Others will be quick to show you your sin, as well. But don't allow them to put more on you than the Lord has given you to bear. If you do, you'll become overwhelmed. The religious leaders weighed the people down so heavily with laws of their own, that there was no way they could succeed. We are free in Jesus. Not enslaved. Separate yourself from those who weigh you down with guilt and shame. If you look at them closely, you might just see that their sin is greater than yours. Perhaps they've busied themselves pointing out the sin of others to take their minds off of their own sin.

Let's look at an example of this very thing.

John 8:3-11

³ The scribes and the Pharisees *brought a woman caught in adultery, and having set her in the center *of the court*, ⁴ they *said to Him, "Teacher, this woman has been caught in adultery, in the very act. ⁵ Now in the Law Moses commanded us to stone such women; what then do You say?" ⁶ They were saying this, testing Him, so that they might have grounds for accusing Him. But Jesus stooped down and with His finger wrote on the ground. ⁷ But when they persisted in asking Him, He straightened up, and said to them, "He who is without sin among you, let him *be the* first to throw a stone at her." ⁸ Again He stooped down and wrote on the ground. ⁹ When they heard it, they *began* to go out one by one, beginning with the older

ones, and He was left alone, and the woman, where she was, in the center *of the court.* **¹⁰ Straightening up, Jesus said to her, "Woman, where are they? Did no one condemn you?" ¹¹ She said, "No one, Lord." And Jesus said, "I do not condemn you, either. Go. From now on sin no more."**

We don't know what the Lord wrote on the ground. Perhaps it was the Ten Commandments, or maybe it was their names, along with their sin. We do know that the Lord was not pleased with them. They were sinners themselves. Instead of confessing their own sin, they were proclaiming the woman's for all to hear.

When we judge others, it is a sign of sin in our own lives. It is always easier to point out someone else's sin, than to take the time to deal with our own. Do yourself a favor and don't get caught up in this. When you find yourself judging others, ask the Lord what sin in your own life needs to be dealt with.

Jesus said in the Sermon on the Mount:

Matthew 7:5

⁵ "You hypocrite, first take the log out of your own eye, and then you will see clearly to take the speck out of your brother's eye.

Remember, Jesus loves the sinner but hates the sin. The Holy Spirit is with us and will see us through to completion. Jesus is saying to us, "I do not condemn you, either. Go. From now on, sin no more."

It Is Well With My Soul

When peace, like a river, attendeth my way,
When sorrows like sea billows roll;
Whatever my lot, Thou has taught me to say,
It is well, it is well, with my soul.

Refrain

It is well, with my soul,
It is well, with my soul,
It is well, it is well, with my soul.

Though Satan should buffet, though trials should come,
Let this blest assurance control,
That Christ has regarded my helpless estate,
And hath shed His own blood for my soul.

Refrain

My sin, oh, the bliss of this glorious thought!
My sin, not in part but the whole,
Is nailed to the cross, and I bear it no more,
Praise the Lord, praise the Lord, O my soul!

Refrain

For me, be it Christ, be it Christ hence to live:
If Jordan above me shall roll,
No pang shall be mine, for in death as in life
Thou wilt whisper Thy peace to my soul.

Refrain

But, Lord, 'tis for Thee, for Thy coming we wait,
The sky, not the grave, is our goal;
Oh trump of the angel! Oh voice of the Lord!
Blessèd hope, blessèd rest of my soul!

Refrain

And Lord, haste the day when my faith shall be sight,
The clouds be rolled back as a scroll;
The trump shall resound, and the Lord shall descend,
Even so, it is well with my soul.

Refrain

Written by: Horatio G. Spafford

DAY 21

SANCTIFICATION

Sanctification: an act of sanctifying;
the state of being sanctified;
Sanctify: to set apart to a sacred purpose or
to a religious use; to free from sin; purify;
Purify: to make pure.

We are going to end by looking at the process of sanctification.

We left Israel bitterly weeping over their sin. Let's see what they've decided to do about it.

Ezra 10:2-4

2 Shecaniah the son of Jehiel, one of the sons of Elam, said to Ezra, "We have been unfaithful to our God and have married foreign women from the peoples of the land; yet now there is hope for Israel in spite of this. 3 So now let us make a covenant with our God to put away all the wives and their children, according to the counsel of my lord and of those who tremble at the commandment of our God; and let it be done according to the law. 4 Arise! For *this* matter is your responsibility, but we will be with you; be courageous and act."

Remember, the law of intermarrying with another race was for

Israel only. This separation was necessary, regardless of how painful and hurtful it was. Their foreign wives knew from the beginning that they didn't belong there. This was their way of entrance. Remember, the foreigners of the land were Israel's enemies. If we think back for a moment, to when they were first rebuilding the temple, we see that these same people tried to get in by offering to help. However, Israel was wise and said no. Now, they've let their defenses down and quit using discernment. As a result, their enemies have gained entrance through their daughters. Their foreign wives were not the only ones that entered. They brought their families with them.

Shecaniah confesses their sin to Ezra and offers to make a covenant with God. They will put away their wives and children, according to the counsel of Ezra and those who feared God and according to the law. He is acting out of humility. He is sincere. He submits himself and the others to Ezra's authority by saying, "We will be with you." He encourages Ezra to be courageous and act.

Ezra 10:5

⁵ Then Ezra rose and made the leading priests, the Levites and all Israel, take oath that they would do according to this proposal; so they took the oath.

Ezra was not willing to do anything until he knew that everyone there was going to fully support this proposal. He made them take an oath. He knew that without unity, his efforts would be a waste of time.

Ezra 10:6-8

⁶ Then Ezra rose from before the house of God and went into the chamber of Jehohanan the son of Eliashib. Although he went there, he did not eat bread nor drink water, for he was mourning over the unfaithfulness of the exiles. ⁷ They made a proclamation

throughout Judah and Jerusalem to all the exiles, that they should assemble at Jerusalem, ⁸ and that whoever would not come within three days, according to the counsel of the leaders and the elders, all his possessions should be forfeited and he himself excluded from the assembly of the exiles.

Ezra got up and went into Jehohanan's chamber, inside the temple, and continued to fast and mourn. A proclamation was sent to all of the exiles, giving them three days to assemble in Jerusalem. Those who wouldn't come would be excluded from the assembly and would forfeit all of their possessions. They would no longer be allowed to come and defile the congregation with their sin.

Ezra 10:9-12

⁹ So all the men of Judah and Benjamin assembled at Jerusalem within the three days. It was the ninth month on the twentieth of the month, and all the people sat in the open square *before* the house of God, trembling because of this matter and the heavy rain. ¹⁰ Then Ezra the priest stood up and said to them, "You have been unfaithful and have married foreign wives adding to the guilt of Israel. ¹¹ Now therefore, make confession to the LORD God of your fathers and do His will; and separate yourselves from the peoples of the land and from the foreign wives." ¹² Then all the assembly replied with a loud voice, "That's right! As you have said, so it is our duty to do.

This was a very difficult and painful time. Their poor choices caused an enormous amount of grief for everyone involved. However, Ezra truly blessed them by boldly confronting them. He did not allow the huge number he was up against to keep him from doing what was necessary in order to get Israel back in right standing with God. This was his responsibility as priest and having been sent by the king. He was not a blind guide. He saw the sin and confronted

225

it head on, bringing it to an end. They were to confess to the Lord their God and do His will, not their own. They were to separate themselves from their foreign wives. The people responded wisely. They took responsibility for their sin and removed it, which was their spiritual duty.

The book of Ezra ends with a list of the names of those who had taken foreign wives. Many of them were the priests and Levites to whom the people were looking as examples. This is why it is so important to follow Jesus and not men. There will always be sinners among and over us. There will always be those who don't take their walk with the Lord as seriously as they should. So be careful not to let them pull you away from doing what is right in the sight of the Lord. Be steadfast in your process of sanctification. Persevere, for your reward is great.

We can no longer tolerate people-pleasing pastors, blind guides who are just as involved in sin as the people are. Through the media, we have all witnessed pastors falling to sin. They are supposed to be leading us on the path of righteousness. We need strong leadership in the church pastors who will confront sin head on. They need to take responsibility for their position by removing sin from the church through repentance and exclusion.

The moment we are born again, we become a holy sanctuary for the Holy Spirit. Therefore, we are sanctified.

II Corinthians 1:21-22

²¹ Now He who establishes us with you in Christ and anointed us is God, ²² who also sealed us and gave *us* the Spirit in our hearts as a pledge.

God is the One who establishes us in Christ. He anoints us with His power to fulfill His purpose in our lives. He gave us the Holy Spirit, who sets us apart from the world. The Holy Spirit is the seal, God's stamp of approval, on our lives for receiving Jesus as our Lord and Savior. God has sealed us as a pledge for the promise of eternal life.

Once we are born again, the process of sanctification begins. During this process, we become more and more like Jesus on a day-to-day basis. It is an ongoing process which will continue until the day we get to Heaven, and God's grace will uphold us throughout. We are to be merciful and compassionate toward each other. We are to pray for those in bondage. Jesus is our Deliverer. He will deliver us from all bondage. At the same time, we are not to allow those who are blatantly sinning inside the church to remain with us. This is hard to do, but it is necessary.

Let's read what the apostle Paul had to say about sanctification.

II Corinthians 6:14-18

14 Do not be bound together with unbelievers; for what partnership have righteousness and lawlessness, or what fellowship has light with darkness? 15 Or what harmony has Christ with Belial, or what has a believer in common with an unbeliever? 16 Or what agreement has the temple of God with idols? For we are the temple of the living God; just as God said,

"I WILL DWELL IN THEM AND WALK AMONG THEM; AND I WILL BE THEIR GOD, AND THEY SHALL BE MY PEOPLE.

17 "Therefore, COME OUT FROM THEIR MIDST AND BE SEPARATE," says the Lord.
"AND DO NOT TOUCH WHAT IS UNCLEAN;
And I will welcome you.

18 "And I will be a father to you,
And you shall be sons and daughters to Me,"
Says the Lord Almighty.

Although we do not separate ourselves by nationality, as Christians, we are not to partner with unbelievers. We have become the righteousness of God, the light of the world and the temple of the living God. We have nothing in common with those who are still under Satan's curse. There is no harmony between us. We don't agree on how things are to be done. We are day and night.

God, through the Holy Spirit, dwells within us and walks among us, as was prophesied. He is our God. We are His people. Therefore, we are to be separate from the world and those in it. We are not to touch what is unclean. When we have accomplished this, He will welcome us and be a Father to us, and we will be His sons and daughters.

Once we become Christians, we cannot go on with life as usual and wonder why we are not receiving His blessings. Being separate from the world is part of the sanctification process. Because we live according to a higher standard, we would be facing a constant battle if we were to marry or go into business with an unbeliever. We line everything up to Christ; they don't.

If we accept Christ as our Lord and Savior while married, we are to win our spouse to the Lord through His love. We are not to divorce our spouse. They have not changed. They are the same people we fell in love with. We are to be more loving to them than ever before, since we now have the love of Christ abiding within us. Don't forget that you once were a sinner, as well. Be merciful and full of grace. Through the love of Christ, you will win them to the Lord.

I Thessalonians 4:1-12

¹ Finally then, brethren, we request and exhort you in the Lord Jesus, that as you received from us *instruction* as to how you ought to walk and please God (just as you actually do walk), that you excel still more. ² For you know what commandments we gave you by

the authority of the Lord Jesus. ³ For this is the will of God, your sanctification; *that is*, that you abstain from sexual immorality; ⁴ that each of you know how to possess his own vessel in sanctification and honor, ⁵ not in lustful passion, like the Gentiles who do not know God; ⁶ *and* that no man transgress and defraud his brother in the matter because the Lord is *the* avenger in all these things, just as we also told you before and solemnly warned *you*. ⁷ For God has not called us for the purpose of impurity, but in sanctification. ⁸ So, he who rejects *this* is not rejecting man but the God who gives His Holy Spirit to you.

⁹ Now as to the love of the brethren, you have no need for *anyone* to write to you, for you yourselves are taught by God to love one another; ¹⁰ for indeed you do practice it toward all the brethren who are in all Macedonia. But we urge you, brethren, to excel still more, ¹¹ and to make it your ambition to lead a quiet life and attend to your own business and work with your hands, just as we commanded you, ¹² so that you will behave properly toward outsiders and not be in any need.

Paul is reminding the church in Thessalonica to abstain from sexual immorality and to control their bodies in sanctification and honor. He adds that no man is to defraud his brother this way, and goes on to say that is because "the Lord is the avenger in all these things." This is a reminder of the wrath of God, and that we have not been called by God for the purpose of impurity, but in sanctification. Those who reject this teaching are rejecting God. Paul ends by saying, "Excel in your love for the brethren. Make it your ambition to lead a quiet life, mind you own business and work with your hands. Then you will behave properly toward outsiders and not be in need of anything." Paul was warning them not to push God to wrath.

Our sanctification is the will of the Lord. The church is the bride of Christ and is to be holy and true to Him. The Lord is coming for His bride and she needs to purify herself. She is to set herself apart from the world, from all that has a grip on her. The church has acted like an unfaithful wife, completely entwined with the world.

The church is to be a place of reverence, holiness, purity, unity, humility and love. Instead, we often find her competing with the world in her appearance, music and activities. Modesty is rarely taught. There is even worldly chatter coming from some pulpits. Some churches have quit modeling reverence, perhaps thinking that not mentioning such things will attract more visitors. In fact, visitors seem to be the only ones who are surprised by the lack of reverence and sanctification inside of these churches. This is shameful. When the leaders of the church no longer model and teach reverence and sanctification, where will it be modeled and taught?

Don't allow yourself to be blinded by pride. No one is above reproach. Sin will steal your blessings. Persevere and separate yourself from anything or anyone that keeps you from God's best. There is peace when we are no longer pulled in every direction by the things of the world. That is when we clearly see what is important to Him and hear His voice louder than ever before. We don't have to be concerned about leading someone in the wrong direction, because we are going in the right direction. We are no longer a stumbling block to others, because we have intentionally removed everything that could cause someone to stumble. We no longer desire the things of the world, let alone crave them.

Jesus is love. He poured out His love when He died on the cross for us. It is a pure love that comes directly from Him. The more like Jesus we become, the more abundant His love is in our lives. Then with a true heart, we will love the unlovely, simply because He first loved us. All that we have and all that we are, becomes His. We should desire nothing less than to use it all for His glory and His kingdom.

I want to end by praying for you as Paul prayed for his disciples.

Philippians 1:6, 9-11

⁶ For I am confident of this very thing, that He who began a good work in you will perfect it until the day of Christ Jesus.

And this I pray, that your love may abound still more and more in real knowledge and all discernment, ¹⁰ so that you may approve the things that are excellent, in order to be sincere and blameless until the day of Christ; ¹¹ having been filled with the fruit of righteousness which *comes* through Jesus Christ, to the glory and praise of God.

Thank you for joining me on this incredible journey. Let God bless and restore you in every area of your life. This is the desire of His heart.

Take My Life and Let It Be

Take my life, and let it be consecrated, Lord, to Thee.
Take my moments and my days; let them flow in ceaseless praise.
Take my hands, and let them move at the impulse of Thy love.
Take my feet, and let them be swift and beautiful for Thee.

Take my voice, and let me sing always, only, for my King.
Take my lips, and let them be filled with messages from Thee.
Take my silver and my gold; not a mite would I withhold.
Take my intellect, and use every power as Thou shalt choose.

Take my will, and make it Thine; it shall be no longer mine.
Take my heart, it is Thine own; it shall be Thy royal throne.
Take my love, my Lord, I pour at Thy feet its treasure store.
Take myself, and I will be ever, only, all for Thee.

Written by: Frances R. Havergal

Need
additional
copies?

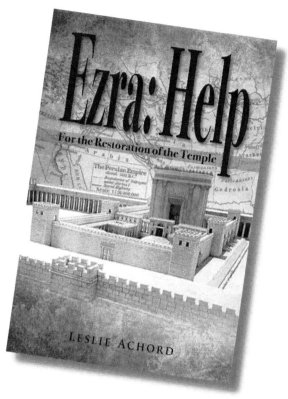

To order more copies of

Ezra: Help

contact NewBookPublishing.com